By the Neck Until Dead:

The Gallows of Nuremberg

By Stanley Tilles

with

Jeff Denhart

JoNa Books
Bedford, Indiana

ISBN 0-9657929-2-7

Library of Congress Number

First Printing August 1999

By the Neck Until Dead:

The Gallows of Nuremberg

Dedicated to all those, both victims and liberators, who lost their lives during the horrendous period of the twentieth century.

Contents:

Author in Munich 1946.

CHAPTER ONE

The Beginning

I was born July 20, 1918, in Boston, Massachusetts. My father, Manuel Tilles, was a printer, and his father, Solomon Tilles, was a book binder that had emigrated from Austria in the first part of the twentieth century. My mother's family, who acquired the name Castleman as a result of a misunderstanding at Elliame by which I have always been known. I understand that I delighted my parents.

A few months after my birth, Adolph Hitler was ending his service in World War I which he termed, "the greatest of all experiences." During his greatest of all experiences, Hitler served in the 16th Bavarian Reserve Regiment that had been continually stationed at the Western Front. He participated in the three major, and bloodiest, battles of the war, Ypres, Somme, and Arras. He received five decorations, including the Iron Cross First Class, and he was wounded three times. He saw death in proportions that had been previously unknown. Forty thousand Germans were killed at Ypres alone, and by the end of the war Hitler's regiment had lost over its numerical strength of nearly 4,000 men, which was not exceptional for a front line unit. Bodies of soldiers were stacked like cord wood and most were buried in mass graves of unprecedented size, which were precursors to concentration camp scenes two decades later. Some historians believe that the exposure to mass death on the battlefield inured Hitler and other Nazis and allowed them to commit the social ravages in World War II.

By 1919 while I was still being suckled at my mother's breast, William II was exiled, and Germany capitulated to the punitive Treaty of Versailles and began to pay reparations. Numerous political parties sprung up in the unstable German society. Hitler was attracted to the National Socialist German Workers Party, later called the Nazi Party, which found most of its support in Bavaria. Hitler assumed a leadership position in the party; Hermann Goering and Heinrich Himmler became his colleagues.

Over the next four years I learned to talk, walk, ride a tricycle, count, recite the alphabet, and write my name. I was still a delight to my parents.

During those same four years the war reparations destroyed Germany's economy, and it suffered what could be termed a civil war or a revolution. The political right found its power through the Freikorps (Free Corps), so called because they were not legally allied to the government, but commanded by officers from World War I. Most of the Freikorps members were Frontkampfers (front fighters, those that served on the front in the war), a group to which Hitler belonged. The Freikorps were enlisted by the German business community to stop the political left from instituting socialist and communistic reforms. Violence between the groups was commonplace. In 1920 Gustav Kapp, a Freikorp member, attempted a coup, which became known as the Kapp Putsch, an action that was not lost on Hitler. Three years later Hitler attempted his own coup, known as the Munich Putsch or the Beerhall Putsch. In hopes of appeasing the German army, who were required to stop any such uprisings, Hitler convinced General Ludendorff, dictator of the Reich in World War I and National Socialist member, to march beside him. In what could be a metaphor and a harbinger of the German condition, the army parted to allow the passage of General Ludendorff, but shot at Hitler and the rest of the marchers. Hitler fell flat in the street to avoid the bullets and ran. He was arrested two days later and sentenced to Landsberg Prison where he wrote Mein Kampf (My Battle). When he was not writing, he could look out his cell window which afforded a view of the courtyard, where twenty-three years later it would contain gallows to hang twenty-eight of Hitler's cohorts.

In 1924 I was in grade school, Hitler was released from prison, and the political climate in Germany had calmed. Hitler noted this and modified the philosophy of the Nazis to discourage putsches and promote organization and discipline. In the next few years, as Germany moved toward depression and its unemployment increased, the Nazi Party, using the promise of a square meal, signed on thousands of jobless men as Storm Troopers, or brown shirts.

The depression affected my family as well. My father's work was cut to two days a week, and in 1929 he left the C.H. Simonds Company where he had worked for over ten years to join the A.S. Browne Company in Newark, New Jersey, where we subsequently moved. I acquired a hand printing press, and I printed small items such as business cards. I earned a few dollars doing this, and I learned some of the values of business.

Hitler may have learned some of the same business values. The socialist aspects of the National Socialist party were forgotten which made it appealing to German business men. The Nazis soon became the largest party in the Reichstag, Germany's parliamentary body. In 1932 the party took a downward slide. Their treasury was depleted, and they had lost seats in the last election. Hitler turned to the business community for support and was not disappointed. A coalition of business men, including Fritz Thyssen, Richard and Eugen Benz, and Curt von Schroeder, paid the Nazis debts and guaranteed wages for the Storm Troopers. In return, Hitler agreed to allow businesses to continue unfettered. Unquestionably, this paved the way to his chancellorship.

In 1933 my family moved to North Bergen, New Jersey, and I started school at Emerson High School in nearby Union

City. I joined the Antlers, or Junior Elks, and with new contacts the demand for my business cards increased.

1933 was an important year for Hitler. His business allies pressured President von Hindenburg to appoint him chancellor, and Hitler was formally installed as such in a lavish ceremony at Potsdam Church where coronations for Prussian kings had been held for centuries. The business community supported Hitler because of his agreement not to regulate or investigate business practices and because he was viewed as a person who could be controlled. Hitler wasted no time in proving the latter perception to be false. He referred to his government as the Third Reich, after the Holy Roman Empire and Bismarck's Empire, called himself Fuhrer (supreme ruler) and passed the Enabling Acts, which gave him power to rule by decree and destroyed any remaining vestiges of democracy. As a youth in Vienna, Hitler had developed anti-Semitic ideas which became more virulent as the years passed. By the time he was chancellor, he firmly believed that Jews had contaminated Germany and were causing its downfall. He called for a boycott of all Jewish businesses and established Dachau and Buchenwald concentration camps for political dissidents, most of whom were Jews.

In 1934 I, along with two friends, drove a Model T Ford touring car to Atlantic City to participate in an Elks parade. We paid five dollars for the car, and it lacked a top, windshield, and most of its floorboards. It rained constantly on the trip, and we huddled under rain coats and used goggles to see the road. Nonetheless, we made the trip and provided one of the two cars in the parade. It remains one of my fondest memories of high school.

Hitler solidified his power in 1934. On the night of the Long Knives or the Roehm Purge, he removed all his political enemies either by execution or by incarceration in concentration camps. Among those that perished was former Chancellor Kurt von Schleicher. Others included Storm Troopers and Freikorps members that were led by Ernst Roehm who had become Hitler's opponent. The executions were carried out by his own elite guard who were distinguished by their black shirts as opposed to the brown shirts worn by the Storm Troopers. This guard became known as the SS, and, with the removal of the Storm Troopers, it began to grow in size and importance. Himmler commanded the SS, and its members were placed in charge of concentration camps. The Gestapo (secret police) which had been formed in 1933 by Goering as a political police unit in Prussia, came under the direction of Himmler. Shortly after the purge of the Storm Troopers and Freikorps members President von Hindenburg died, and Hitler named himself president and combined the offices of chancellor and president. By the end of the year Hitler essentially had no opposition in Germany.

By 1935 my printing business had increased to the point that, for a high school student, I was making a fair amount of money. I decided to expand, and I invested in a used electric press which I set up in the basement of my parent's home. I continued to print business cards and soon secured a contract to print liquor labels for a local applejack producer.

My modest success contrasted the plight of Jews in Germany. Hitler's boycott severely hurt Jewish business men and many lost their businesses. The Nuremberg Laws were issued in 1935 which forbade Jews to intermarry with Aryans and deprived them of civil service positions. Hitler chose Nuremberg as his forum because he revered its German history and because Nuremberg lay in Bavaria, an anti-Semitic region not likely to question such racist laws.

In 1936 I graduated from high school and went to work at A. S. Brown Printing Company in Hoboken, New Jersey, where my father was a supervisor. My family and I enjoyed several successes over the next couple of years. My father's hard work had advanced us to the economic level of middle class, and he had a house built in Teaneck, New Jersey in 1938. That same year I married Jeane Manett, who remained my wife for over fifty years, and we settled into an apartment in Englwood, New Jersey, not far from the site of the Lindbergh kidnapping.

Hitler also had successes. In 1936 he remilitarized the Rhineland and waited for a reaction from European leaders. When none came, he annexed Austria and divided Czechoslovakia. At the Munich Conference in 1938 he justified his actions to the European diplomats and came away without reprimand. His domestic policies continued to be severe for Jews. He decreed that the Gestapo was a national secret police and forbade any appeals against its decisions. The Gestapo was to suppress any form of opposition, and it was divided into six sections. The second section dealt with religious opposition, and it subsection four dealt with the Jewish religion. This subsection was headed by Adolph Eichmann who promoted savage torture, murder, and confinement of the Jews. When a Jew killed a German diplomat in 1938, Hitler and the country responded in an anti-Semitic frenzy with the Kristallnacht (Night of the Broken Glass) in which synagogues were destroyed and 20,000 Jews were slaughtered. After Kristallnacht any Jew wishing to emigrate from Germany had to sacrifice all his possessions. Many Jews remained because of this law despite their treatment, and because, at this point, no country, including the United States, would accept Jewish refugees.

The Christian religions fared almost as poorly. Hitler closed all Catholic schools, which he felt threatened the monopoly of his Hitler Youth Organization, and forbade its religious celebrations. Oddly, Hitler himself was a nominal Catholic, and he was impressed by its organizational structure which he occasionally praised in his speeches. He used that structure as a model for his youth groups and the SS. Through the Protestant religions Hitler had hoped to form a state church under the leadership of a Reichbishop. This idea failed when the

14

Protestant pastors resisted. Unable to bring them in line with his thinking, Hitler imprisoned many of the pastors in concentration camps along with the Hews and Catholic priests.

While my wife and I set up housekeeping and adjusted to married life, Hitler invaded Poland in 1939 and started World War II. The following year he invaded Russia. My son, Loren, was born in 1941 not long before Pearl Harbor brought the United States into the war. On December 8, 1941, Hitler declared war on the United States in a show of support for his ally, Japan. Later that month he took command of the German army.

Despite the fact that in a year and a half he had conquered most of Europe, Hitler still anguished over the presence of Jews. Both Poland and Russia had large Jewish populations, and they could not be allowed to taint the Aryans that would inhabit the newly conquered regions. The ghetto of Warsaw was created immediately after Poland's invasion, and as many Jews as possible were confined there. The ghetto was created on Yom Kippur, 1940, and a half a million Jews confined to two and a half square miles of the oldest part of Warsaw; starvation and epidemics of all types were prevalent. By July of 1942, most of the ghetto residents were shipped by cattle cars to Treblinka and ultimately to its gas chamber. His treatment of the Russian Jews and those in rural Poland was more brutal. Einsatzgruppen (death squads) that were composed of SS and Gestapo troops, were dispatched with explicit orders to kill Jews; 33,771 were slaughtered in the Barbi Yav raid at Kiev. Hitler toyed with the idea of deporting all Jews to Madagascar, but in 1942, a group of intellectuals under the direction of SS General Reinhard Heydrich met at what became known as the Wannsee Conference. They decided that deportation was impractical and that confinement in concentration camps and sporadic slaughters were insufficient. The Final Solution was proposed, and the systematic elimination of Jews began. The method of execution was also chosen at the conference. To that point Jews had been slaughtered either by being herded into a ditch that they had dug themselves and then machine gunned to death or by being suffocated by carbon monoxide from a truck engine. Neither method had proved to be efficient. Some of those who were machine gunned managed to dig themselves out of their mass graves which caused civic leaders to complain to the SS. To prevent this it was necessary for the soldiers to wade ankle deep in blood and entrails and kill any survivors before the ditch was covered. This had a deleterious effect on the soldiers, and many relied heavily on alcohol and developed stress related conditions. The slaughters by carbon monoxide were not much better. It took considerable time to suffocate the victims, and the soldiers were subjected to their death throes. There were frequently survivors that the soldiers had to kill individually. At Wannsee a scientist suggested that the use of potassium cyanide was a more effective death agent. The suggestion was approved because the execution process would require less time and the soldiers would have less exposure to their victims and their final agonies. The use of cyanide would be more human for the executioners; the victims' feelings were inconsequential. Although cyanide was championed by the members of the conference, General Heydrich still allowed the alternate methods to be used in some camps under the philosophy that competition for the highest death rates among the camps led to increased efficiency.

In 1942, I bought a house in Bergenfield, New Jersey, and Germany was at the height of its power. Although we heard reports of German U-boats off our coast and several American freighters had been sunk, my wife and I, along with most of the rest of America, felt safe. We had confidence in our armed forces, and we contributed as much as possible to the war effort. I served as an air raid warden for my neighborhood, and my wife dealt with the various rations. Our lives were basically unscathed. I worked, usually long hours because of the shortage of help, and Jeane raised our son and maintained our home. If

16

our families had chosen to stay in Europe, we would not have been safe, nor would we have had a home or possessions. We probably wouldn't have been able to marry and wouldn't have had a son. Even though we didn't regularly practice the Jewish faith, we still would have been hunted by the Gestapo and placed in a concentration camp where, depending on the type of labor we were forced to do, we might survive a month or a year. Or we could have been executed outright.

CHAPTER TWO

Drafted

In December of 1944, I was twenty-six years old and had been married six years. I had a three year old son, a good job, mortgage payments, and because of my age, family responsibilities, and a less than average physical condition, I hadn't been drafted. Occasionally, I felt a little sad that I had missed out on the excitement and adventure of war, and sometimes I felt a little guilty for not being actively involved in the defense of my country. Mostly, I felt overwhelming relief that my life was intact and uninterrupted. I had been called to the induction center eight months earlier and was told I'd be called only if needed. By December with the Allied armies invading Germany and with the Japanese losing island after island in the Pacific, it was widely believed that the war was nearly over, and I was certain I'd never be called. I anticipated a joyful Christmas and world peace in the new year.

A few days before Christmas the postman presented me with my draft notice. I was to report on January 3, 1945. Jeane was inconsolable. Loren, my son, was not old enough to understand what war was but knew that his mother was upset. My prediction that I wouldn't pass the physical did little to mitigate their anxiety. I've never quite forgiven the army for ruining that Christmas season for my family.

On January 3rd, contrary to my prediction, I passed my physical and was sworn in at Fort Dix, New Jersey, and given the task of firing the barrack's coal furnace. Two days later I was transported by train to Camp Robinson, Arkansas, and assigned to "D" Company, Fourth Platoon.

Basic training nearly killed me. I was, by army standards, old, certainly lacking the energy, strength, and stamina of the eighteen year olds that had passed before me. I survived only because the rest of the recruits were, like me, drafted late in the war because we were far from soldier material. I'm sure the DI's lowered their expectations as they watched us puff our way through calisthenics and around the obstacle course.

About two weeks before my basic training ended interviews were held for Officer Candidate School. Figuring that being an officer would involve less physical and less dangerous activities, I signed up, passed a number of tests, and was interviewed by a board of officers. I was accepted and shipped to Fort Benning, Georgia for training. The physical training was still tough, but I excelled at the academic classes.

Before I started by training Germany surrendered on May 8, 1945, V-E Day. During my training the Japanese surrendered on September 2, 1945. I was positive that I would be sent home directly, and until that happened, I was secure in the fact that I wouldn't be in combat.

My elation was short lived. I was informed, along with the rest of the candidates, that we would be taking the place of the soldiers that were coming home. I graduated a second lieutenant and received my gold bars on September 27, 1945, and I was assigned as a training instructor with the 24th Company, 3rd Student Training Regiment. This was the next best thing to being discharged; I had stateside duty and could live with my family off base.

The army is never happy to leave a soldier alone, especially if he might be happy. On the very day my wife and son were to join me, I received orders to report to Camp Picket and prepare for my assignment in Germany.

My wife was again upset and tearful. I tried to get my orders changed, but I couldn't. In the days before I shipped out I consoled her by telling her that the war was over and I couldn't possibly become involved in anything dangerous or important.

CHAPTER THREE

Dachau

My journey to Europe began on a troop ship packed with men charged with the same task as I -- to replace the soldiers that had fought in the European theater and to become part of Germany's occupying army. We were going to a country that could best be described as chaotic. Germany lacked a central government, and its leaders had fled, committed suicide, or been arrested. It had been divided among the Allied powers, but each had different motivations. England and the United States, which occupied the northwest and southwest sections, were interested in the de-Nazification of the German people, providing economic stability, and establishing local governments that were run by non-Nazi leaders. France occupied a small portion of Germany next to its border and wanted reparations. The Soviets, who occupied the eastern section, wanted huge reparations, the land they had secured at the end of the war, for their sector of Germany to become part of the Soviet system, and to create a barrier between itself and the rest of Europe. The Soviets displayed interest in Germany's art, culture, literature, and architecture, and they looted anything that could be moved from their section.

By some estimates there were nine million displaced persons in Germany; indeed it took over five years to resettle all of them. Such persons included German P.O.W.'s, concentration camp survivors, refugees from the eastern section that the Soviets had expelled, as well as German citizens whose homes had been destroyed in bombing raids. Many lived in tents and barracks abandoned by the army; others in cellars and in the rubble of bombed out buildings. Disease and malnutrition were rampant. Black marketeering and prostitution flourished. A pack of American cigarettes was worth as much as thirty dollars; nylons were priceless. They were so valuable that American soldiers had pairs mailed to them from the states. A single pair could get a soldier a woman for several days.

The vast majority of Germans were relieved that the fighting had stopped and did not overtly resist the occupying forces. German P.O.W.'s, even the elite SS Troops, were docile as long as they were fed. There was some sporadic resistance, and before the war ended the Nazis began a rumor that SS Troops would hide in the Bavarian forests and continue to fight. These troops were called Werewolves by Hitler and others. (Hitler seemed fascinated by the name "Wolf." His code name throughout the war was Wolf, and he named two of his headquarters Wolf's Gorge and Wolf's Camp). The Werewolves proved more rumor than fact, although some American soldiers were subjected to sniper fire as they drove through the country side, and a few were decapitated by wires that stretched across roads. The army solved the latter threat by welding three feet of sharpened angle iron to the front of all jeeps.

The allies agreed that German war criminals needed to be punished. Churchill suggested that they be shot on sight; the United States argued for trials with the rationale that making their crimes and punishments public would act as a future deterrent. Such trials were held throughout Germany; most defendants were concentration camp operators. The trials were usually short; the punishment was usually death by hanging. The Nuremberg Trial, the centerpiece of allied justice, was commencing as I sailed toward Germany.

I arrived at LeHavre, France, but before I could enjoy solid ground, I was trucked to Etretat. There I was placed, along with other junior officers, in a freight car for a four day trip by rail to the replacement depot at Erlangen, Germany.

Erlangen began my German odyssey. For whatever reason or perversion, the army seemed disinclined to allow me to settle anywhere. Two days after my arrival at the replacement depot, I was sent to Bad Tolz in the German Alps. I was billeted, along with many others, in a resort hotel. It was winter and frightfully cold, but the hotel afforded spectacular views and some remnants of old world luxury. It was there that I saw my first bidet. Actually, I was among the few sophisticates that had heard of a bidet. Many of the soldiers were baffled by the seemingly backward rush of water.

On December 11, 1945, I received my first assignment which was the Sixth Tank Destroyer Group at Dachau. The name "Dachau" typed in smudged carbon on my orders chilled me more than the winter winds that whipped through the Alps.

Dachau is in Bavaria in Southern Germany about ten miles from Munich, and it was settled as a market city during the reign of Charlemagne around 800 A.D. At the time of World War II it was still primarily an agricultural city in a rural setting, although it had such domestic industries as breweries and textile mills. It had not been considered a military target and had escaped bomb damage. Perhaps because of its rural setting and perhaps because the civic leaders of Dachau offered Himmler the use of an empty munitions plant, the Nazis established their first concentration camp in 1933 just outside the city. The citizens of Dachau thought of the camp as a boon to their local economy; craftsmen and merchants made considerable money supplying building materials and constructing the barracks. Dachau's concentration camp became a system of one main camp and eighty-five branch or subsidiary camps, a pattern typical to all concentration camps. At the time of its liberation the main camp held 33,000 prisoners; the prisoners in the branch camps totaled 65,000. It's estimated that Dachau housed over a half a million prisoners in its twelve year existence, and over 100,000 lost their lives in ways that stagger the imagination.

Despite these numbers Dachau was probably one of the better camps in terms of conditions for prisoners. A diary entry written by one prisoner stated that "Dachau is a golden camp." The SS had official classifications for concentration camps. Dachau was Grade I and was for persons "in need of special consideration" and "prisoners with good records." Auschwitz was a Grade II camp, "for those likely to benefit from education and reform." Grade III camps for "those who cannot be reeducated" included Mauthausen, Majdanek, and Treblinka and were specifically death camps. Dachau was started a political camp, and its first prisoners were Communists, Social Democrats, and monarchists, all of whom opposed Hitler. Jews were soon determined to be political enemies as well as an inferior race contaminating the German people and they were imprisoned. They were followed by Jehovah's Witnesses, who resisted the draft, Gypsies, who were also thought to be contaminants, clergymen who offered resistance, and homosexuals. As the war progressed many foreigners, especially Poles, were imprisoned at Dachau. The camp did not have a gas chamber until one was built inside the new crematorium in 1942. The gas chamber, however, was never used. Prisoners that were to be gassed were shipped to Hartheim Castle in Linz, Austria, the site of a former insane asylum.

The fact that the gas chamber was unused did not eliminate mass death at Dachau. Medical experiments, particularly the altitude and freezing experiments of Dr. Sigmund Rasher and the malaria experiments by Dr. Karl Klaus Schilling, claimed hundreds of lives. The camp started a euthanasia program in 1941. Dachau prisoners were shipped to various factories and mines for forced labor. Any prisoner who became too sick or weak to work was eliminated by starvation. Those to be starved were placed in rooms separate from the other prisoners. Most were too weak from exhaustion and illness to get up or protest. Their bodies soon withered and dehydrated into shapes that more resembled long elephant tusks than human forms. A typhus epidemic raged through the camp toward the end of the war and probably took thousands of lives. Death was so common that despite constant use of the crematorium and mass graves, it was impossible to dispose of all the bodies.

When it became obvious that the war was lost, the operators of Dachau received orders to kill all prisoners and dispose of the bodies and any evidence of the Germans' improper activities. The operators followed the order; American soldiers found many piles of bodies, most of which had been shot. The bodies had not been neatly stacked as those were by the crematorium, but thrown together in a jumble of torsos and limbs. Possibly the piles were to have been burned, but the SS soldiers fled before finishing their task. Poison gas was released in some of the barracks; prisoners were found dead in their bunks. Some had crawled along the floor in a vain attempt to escape. Most of the dead were partially clothed; several men were found with their pants around their ankles which was perhaps an attempt by the SS to deprive the Jews of any final dignity.

In a further attempt to cover their crimes, some 8000 prisoners were force marched out of Dachau southward into the Alps. Most died of exhaustion and exposure. Allied troops reported seeing frozen forms of thousands of bodies outside Bad Tolz. By the time the few survivors were reached, the SS guards had fled. Other prisoners were locked into boxcars to be removed by train. Engines never arrived to move the cars, and the prisoners died from starvation, dehydration, and suffocation. When the Americans broke the cars open over five hundred bloated corpses tumbled from each car.

West gate at Dachau.

I was unprepared for my first sight of the camp. By this time I knew, as did the rest of the world, of the treatment of the concentration camp inmates by the camp operators. The horrors found when the camps were liberated went beyond the limits of what a normal mind can process. No one is prepared to see hundreds, thousands of bodies stacked higher than a man's head, or emaciated prisoners in filthy, bloody rags or wearing nothing, or mass graves with arms and legs poking through the earth, or gas chambers or crematoriums. The stories told by the prisoners were equally disturbing -- death by flogging, butchery, starvation, freezing and scalding, lethal germ injections, and amputations. There was so much horror that it became surreal and my mind conjured an image that it could accept. I was prepared to see some ramshackle barracks, rusted wire fences, and rutted roads, all of which would be on about a half acre of land. Something small and furtive actions of a few sick minds. I was wrong. The camp was anything but tenuous, and it covered more acres than could be seen in a single view. Solid brick structures with several offices served as the gate. Large, three story duplexes outside the main gate housed the officers. Inside the gate were plush houses for the camp operators. The largest part of the camp was behind a double barbed wire fence and was termed "the cage". This has been the inmates' area, and it contained thirty-two wooden barracks, each with eight rooms, and each of those with rows of triple bunks. Each building had contained up to two thousand prisoners with four persons sharing a single bunk. During its operation the cage was surrounded by an electrified fence and a moat. Many prisoners committed suicide by throwing themselves onto the fence. Dachau was bigger than most American cities. It was permanent, solid, self sufficient, and had been part of the German society for twelve years.

Inside the cage, but separate from the barracks, was the crematorium, a modern brick building with a tile roof. Except for the tall chimney at its rear its outward appearance resembled an office building. Its interior, however, didn't. Three brick

27

ovens occupied a spare, concrete room. Long iron hooks used to lift bodies into the ovens and to rake out their ashes and bones adorned the gray walls. Prisoners had been forced to work in the crematorium burning the bodies of their family members and friends. When the camp was liberated bodies were found ringing the outside of the building as well as solidly packed inside the concrete room.

The gas chamber was within the same building as the crematorium but was separate from it. It was disguised as a shower room, but it was never used. The shower baths were at the opposite end of the camp and these were used for torture. The prisoners were herded through a single door that was bolted behind them. The controls for the water were on the outside of the building, and the prisoners were subjected to freezing shards of water followed by scalding steam. The Nazis had windows installed so that they could witness the writhing mass of tortured, naked bodies. Not all prisoners survived this treatment.

By the time I arrived, the camp had most of its evidence of death removed, although pictures were taken to document the conditions. The first priority of the American army was to bury the hundreds of bodies to prevent the spread of disease. Those prisoners that had been covered in mass graves were disinterred and buried properly. German citizens were made to perform the labor for these burials. The graves and the grounds around the crematorium were then blanketed with several inches of lye; nonetheless, I was told that the stench of rotted flesh permeated the camp for weeks.

In what I thought was an appropriate irony, the cage area was now used by the U.S. Army to house some 20,000 German SS prisoners of war, who, from my observation, were provided with infinitely better conditions that the former inhabitants.

I was billeted in what had been German officers' quarters outside the main gate. My room was one of three rooms on the second floor; the other two housed Lieutenants Constantine Zimmermann and Bob Selvidge. A captain resided on the third floor, and he shared his room with a female German concert pianist who played at the officers' mess. A German whose name I remember as Liesl, lived in the attic. She ran the camp switchboard. I met her for the first time on the staircase; she was dressed in a faded frock and ill fitting army combat boots. We exchanged greetings, and she clumped down the stairs in her boots.

This was my first contact with a German citizen, and I soon learned that fraternization with German women, although forbidden, was common, especially among officers. The German people lacked many staples, such as shoes, and would do anything to get them from their captors. For women this meant becoming concubines and prostitutes; men served as laborers for the army in exchange for food and lodging. This situation confused me; a few months before the Germans had been our enemy. I didn't understand why we would accept labor services from our enemy, and I understand less why the Germans would provide it. Of course, I understand the reasons for prostitution, but the behavior of the American soldiers and the German women went beyond the realm of simple prostitution. German women simply made themselves available to American soldiers. Young women took soldiers into their homes with the consent and even encouragement of their mothers. Officers kept women in their quarters, and at Dachau they were allowed to bring the women to the officers' club on weekends. Women traded their favors for a tin of coffee, canned peaches, chocolate, cigarettes, or simply for a warm place to sleep for a night. I didn't understand their willingness, but the practice was ubiquitous, and I soon accepted it.

One weekend Lieutenant Zimmermann, who was the motor pool officer, took advantage of this willingness. He requisitioned a two and a half ton truck, drove to Munich, and waited outside the phone company for the shift to change. As the operators, all females, left for the day, he invited them to a party with Americans. With an offer as slim as that, he returned to our quarters with the truck full of women. Most of the women were grateful for the opportunity to have good food, something to drink, and cigarettes.

I hadn't been in Germany long enough to know the conditions that faced the citizens, but I surmised that they couldn't have been good. An incident confirmed this. On weekends a band played music at the officers' mess during dinner. The musicians were German P.O.W.'s that were housed at a subsidiary camp a few miles to the north, and they were brought to Dachau by truck. One musician learned that his wife, who lived in the city of Dachau, was consorting with an American officer. He slipped away from the band and didn't get on the truck to return to his P.O.W. camp. He made his way into the city of Dachau and dealt with his wife. Apparently, his absence from the camp went unnoticed, and he had successfully escaped. Nonetheless, the following week he rejoined the band, boarded the truck, and returned to the camp. As a P.O.W. he was fed and kept warm and dry, something that he wasn't able to do on his own. Perhaps simple pragmatism explained the behavior of the Germans.

My duties at Dachau involved training the new recruits that were replacing veteran soldiers. Most of these men were under twenty and had had no military experience beyond basic training. Most of the training that I provided was physical, including close order drills and hikes. Because of this, I usually fell into an exhausted sleep every night. Although at times I resented the physical strain of my assignment, I came to regard it as a blessing. I had no time or energy to reflect on the atrocities that had occurred on the very ground on which I walked every day. My duties, I think saved me from being haunted by the thousands of wretched, tortured souls that met their fates at Dachau.

The army at Dachau and throughout Germany was in constant flux with veteran soldiers leaving and recruits arriving daily. Usually more soldiers left than arrived, and the army was short handed. Because of this situation, Polish soldiers were used in several capacities. One of their duties was to guard the SS prisoners, and they occupied the same guard towers that had been used by the SS soldiers, another appropriate irony, The Poles had lost their homes and property, their families, and their country to the Nazis, and their hatred for the SS prisoners was palpable. They did not hesitate to shoot at and sometimes kill any prisoner that approached the "no man's land" that bordered the barbed wire fence. Sometimes they were reprimanded for shooting too quickly, but it didn't have much effect on them.

The army used some of the German prisoners to make up for the man-power shortage. Some were used for mundane tasks; others had positions of responsibility. A German sergeant, who had been in a German motor pool, assisted Lieutenant Zimmermann on a daily basis. During his duties he wore his German uniform with his sergeant stripes, but with all SS insignia removed. Even the SS prisoners displayed a desire to please their captors. Zimmermann's assistant directed him to camp warehouses that contained caches of cigars, SS caps, and fez hats with SS insignia. Such items were more valuable than money among the American soldiers.

Perhaps even the hardened SS troops knew that being imprisoned by the Americans was better than any fate that they would have had with the Soviets. This was illustrated to me about two weeks after my arrival. Housed with the prisoners was a group of 100 Soviets who, before the German invasion of the Soviet Union, has become SS soldiers. During the invasion they had remained loyal to the SS and had fought against their mother country. Now these prisoners were to be transported to the Soviet Union for trial.

By now the relations between the United States and the Soviet Union were disintegrating into what would become the cold war. Our orders were to assist the Soviets with the transport, but not to interfere. When the troop train arrived for the prisoners, I was among the several American soldiers that were positioned directly outside the cage to provide a back up force. A Soviet officer and twenty soldiers, all armed with machine guns, entered the cage. The American Commandant led them to the barracks that housed the prisoners. The prisoners were ordered out in English, German, and Russian, but the order was not obeyed. The Soviet officer ordered his soldiers to enter the barracks. As the men approached, the door burst open, and naked prisoners threw themselves on the ground and begged not to be taken back. The officer ordered them to clothe themselves, but they refused. Finally, he ordered them marched naked to the train. At this point, two American officers entered the cage to confer with the Soviet officer. The prisoners rushed to the Americans and pleaded for mercy. The American officers knew better than to interfere, and quickly left the cage. The prisoners then tried to run in mass to the gate. The Polish guards needed no other excuse to begin firing. The Soviet soldiers also fired a the naked prisoners. Many were hit, but none were killed, and, no matter their conditions, all were loaded on the train to the Soviet Union.

My time at Dachau was blessedly short. In early 1946, Lieutenant Colonel Beall, who was commander of the Sixth Tank Destroyer Group, became an assistant to Colonel Philip Clayton, the Provost Marshal, Third Army. Beall needed officers to assist in his assignment as Prisoner of War and Civilian Internee Officer, and he selected Captain Clyde Arnold and myself to accompany him to Heidelberg. Before I departed, I ventured into the city itself and conversed with several citizens that spoke English. I was curious to know how much they knew about the camp and how they felt about it. Each person I asked, denied any knowledge of the conditions, medical experiments, the tortures, crematorium, or mass graves. They stated that they thought the camp was simply a detention center for laborers. They claimed to have been as shocked as the rest of the world to learn what actually took place inside the camp.

I found this attitude to be common among the Germans. Despite such overwhelming evidence as a continuous procession of railroad cars packed with people, the greasy, black smoke from the crematoriums that covered the city day and night, and the stench of hundreds of rotting bodies too numerous to be buried or burned, the citizens of Dachau insisted that they knew nothing of any improprieties. One theory for this phenomenon was that an anti-Semitic attitude was ingrained in German society, and Jews were regarded as sub human, and thus acceptable to eliminate. Another theory was that obedience to authority was likewise ingrained in the German people; they did what they were told to do. More than one American officer noted that the Germans were easy to work with because they followed orders without questions. An example of this might be the German civilians willingly burying the dead at Dachau while denying knowledge of any mass killings.

CHAPTER FOUR

Heidelberg & Munich

At Heidelberg I was assigned to inspect American P.O.W. and Civilian Internee camps. I was provided with a jeep, a driver, Private Dale Hossman, a trailer full of gasoline cans, and a map, and I was sent into the snow covered country side. I inspected perhaps ten camps in the American Zone which was comprised of the state of Bavaria. This was an area about the size of New Jersey, but the task took me over a week. Many roads were impassable because of bomb damage or snow, and my routes involved much circumnavigation.

My inspections were probably perfunctory and usually involved meeting with the American officer in charge and making a list of the items that he said he required. I heard after I had returned to the states that at the close of the war Americans had allowed German P.O.W.'s to starve and freeze. I saw no evidence of this. The camps I visited seemed clean and orderly, and the few prisoners that I saw were healthy and well fed. The prisoners again displayed a desire to please their captors. I received at least one hand crafted gift from a prisoner at each camp. One gift was an ingenious cigarette dispenser fashioned from wood scraps and rubber bands that is still usable today.

My inspection duties did expose me to the ravages of the war. The ultra modern autobahn, which had been built in the thirties under the guise of a job creation project but which served as both a highway for troop movements and as emergency landing strips for the air force, was largely destroyed. I traveled

34

over some of its few remaining sections, but nearly every bridge had been bombed either by the Allies or by retreating German soldiers. Occasionally, a lone Roman arch protruded from the floor of a valley, a useless remnant of modern engineering.

Ashaffenberg, a camp that I inspected in the northern part of the American zone, portrayed the human devastation that the Nazis had wrought on Europe. The camp was operated by the United Nations Relief and Rehabilitation Association (UNRRA) and held nearly 200,000 people. Most were Poles, who, under Germany's labor policy, were conscripted along with millions of others to supply a labor force. These slave laborers were treated a little better than the Jews and were saved from the gas chambers only by the fact that their labor was deemed necessary to the war effort.

I have never forgotten that camp, and I have never felt so sorry for anyone as I did those people. The camp was hopelessly overcrowded and understaffed, and despite all efforts it was impossible to provide food, medical attention, and sanitation for all 200,000 people. Ten to fifteen people were packed into tiny tents and crude shelters, excrement ran in shallow ditches, food was sharply rationed, and the odor was overwhelming. Unfortunately, many died in the camp while waiting to be returned to Poland, and I've always thought it pitiful that those refuges survived the brutal conditions of the Nazi war machine only to perish when peace was restored.

Heidelberg itself was largely a residential city and had not sustained much bomb damage, which was one of the reasons that it was chosen for Third Army headquarters--plenty of intact buildings. The city was divided by the Neckar River into the old city and the new city. When I had a day off I drove to Heidelberg Castle which sat on a hill overlooking the city and viewed its gothic skyline. I took a picture from the castle, and when I returned to the states, I showed it to our family doctor. He and his wife, who were both Jewish, had lived in Heidelberg until they escaped in the late thirties. They enjoyed seeing their home

35

town and identified several landmarks including their former home.

In March, the Sixth Tank Destroyer Group became part of the Constabulary, which was the army police force for Germany. I was assigned to the Eighth Tank Battalion in Straubing, which became part of the Fifth Constabulary regiment, and I was given the duty of training new recruits. In Straubing I became acquainted with Lieutenant Harry Hillman. He had found a German motorcycle that he managed to get in running condition. We rode through the mountains on the cycle; he drove, and I hung on for dear life behind him.

Anita Thyssen, whose father had financed Hitler and the Nazis in the early thirties, had a mansion near our headquarters. One of the duties of the Constabulary was to protect this mansion, presumable from looters. We had access to the mansion and grounds, and it became the site of weekend parties. We took our own food and drink and lolled around its luxuriously furnished fifty plus rooms.

At the first party that I attended, I succumbed to temptation and acquired three souvenirs. I took a unique book from her library; I was a printer, after all. A chromium bed lamp caught my attention. It had a push button switch, which I had never seen before. I also took a desk blotter, but I can no longer remember why that fascinated me.

Despite such parties and motorcycle tours, I did not want to be part of the Constabulary because I thought it would increase my service time in Germany. I appealed to Lt. Colonel Beall to re-assign me to the Third Army. My next orders did the exact opposite; I was sent to Sonthoffen to take a basic training course for service in the Constabulary. I appealed again, and this time my request was granted. On April 8, 1946, I was again assigned to Heidelberg.

The Provost Marshal's Section was in a state of flux when I arrived. Lt. Colonel Beall went to the states for temporary duty, and Lt. Colonel McLaughlin took his place as assistant to the Provost Marshal. Lt. Colonel Fogarty took charge of the Provost Marshal Section rear in Munich, and he took me with him.

Fogarty gave me the job of registering the private vehicles owned by allied personnel. Because of the reduction in its forces the army had a lot of extra equipment, some of which was available to soldiers through the PX. Jeeps were the most popular item, and they could be purchased for $200 in poor condition, $430 in fair condition, and $800 in good condition. Ranking officers drove elegant Mercedes and Rolls Royces that had been confiscated from Germans. A Tatra, a Czech produced car, was available for use at our headquarters. A Tatra has a rear, air cooled, aluminum V-8 engine, but the one in the car was unusable. A sergeant was able to exchange the engine with one he located in a junk yard, and the car ran like the hammers of hell. The sergeant became enamored of the car and wanted to take it home. Although using German property was permitted, removing it from the country was prohibited. We adjusted the car's paper work to make it Czech property, and the sergeant took it home to Chicago.

My job was less physically demanding than my previous assignments. I enjoyed seeing the different cars, and through a connection at the PX, I purchased a Jeep which I had painted two tone blue. The paint job cost me two packs of American cigarettes. I later had the seats re-upholstered in red material for a similar price. I believed that I could ride out my remaining time with this light duty when I was handed new orders to coordinate the arrangements for the executions at Landsberg.

CHAPTER FIVE

The Hangings at Landsberg

Twenty-eight men were to be executed at Landsberg, and all of them had been operators and guards at the Dachau concentration camp. They had been tried at Dachau itself shortly before my arrival there. (Dachau was the site of many military tribunal trials of war criminals until 1947. A total of 1672 criminals were tried, 1090 were found guilty, and 426 were sentenced to death.) This trial had been convened by the Provost Marshal's Section Third Army; eight army officers sat in judgment, and Brigadier General John Lenz presided. The trial is known as the Dachau Concentration Camp Trial or The Trial of Martin Gottfried Weiss and Thirty-nine Others. Besides Weiss, the commandant, the other defendants included eight camp commandants or deputy commandants, three rapport fuhrers, who were in charge of discipline, four labor officers, five medical officers, two medical orderlies, three members of the administrative staff, four block fuhrers, three guards in charge of prisoner convoys, three prisoner trustees, one officer in charge of the battalion guards, one supply officer, one political officer, and one officer in charge of work patrols. All were charged with "the subjection of civilian nationals of nations then at war with the then German Reich to cruelties and mistreatment, including killings, beatings, tortures, starvation, abuses and indignities..."

Evidence that was presented included photographs of the piles of bodies and mass graves, testimony of survivors who told of beatings, starvation, disease, and hangings, and physical evidence. Some of the physical evidence was particularly appalling. A pile of teeth, so large that it covered a table top with several inches of cracked and shattered molars was presented. Prisoners had been forced to extract the teeth from bodies before they were cremated. The Germans removed any gold dental work. Novelties made from human skin were also displayed. Apparently, such items were status symbols for the SS soldiers, and lamp shades, book covers, and riding breeches were fashioned out of human skin. (Other status symbols including human skulls that were used as hood ornaments.) Tattooed skin was especially valuable, and the skin needed to be free from defects and come from healthy prisoners. When such skin was scarce, Dr. Rascher, who conducted the freezing and altitude experiments, would provide twenty or thirty bodies to be skinned that had been shot in the head thus leaving the skin unblemished.

All forty defendants were found guilty and thirty-four were sentenced to death. In the ensuing months six had their sentences commuted to prison terms by the Reviewing Authority; twenty-eight awaited the rope at Landsberg. While the trial and the sentences did not have the notoriety of the Nuremberg Trial, which had started at about the same time and was currently in its fifth month, Landsberg was the first mass execution attempted by the army. Its success would legitimize the desire of the allies to make war criminals pay for their offenses and verify the United States' belief that the punishment should be determined by public trial.

I became responsible for coordinating this precedent setting execution in typical army fashion. The Provost Marshal Third Army, to which I was assigned, had been responsible for the trial and therefore responsible for the executions. Lt. Colonel Beall, had directed an earlier execution, and thus the task fell to him. Beall was on temporary duty in the states, and the task was passed to Lt. Colonel McLaughlin. McLaughlin logically determined that since Munich was close to Landsberg, Lt. Colonel Fogarty should assume responsibility. Since Fogarty had no desire to perform the task himself, and since I was the lowest ranking and newest officer in his command, the task was passed down to me.

In his briefing Lt. Colonel Fogarty informed me that the actual hangings would be done by Master Sergeant John Woods, who was the official executioner for the army. He was presently in Landsberg supervising the building of a second gallows. With a second gallows, Fogarty explained, the army hoped to cut the time of the executions to two days with seven men to be hung each morning and afternoon. This plan required a second hangman and Colonel Fogarty provided me with the name of a German that Colonel Beall had previously used and told me it was imperative that I find him. He said that one of the German secretaries in his office knew him and suggested that I start my search with her.

The following morning I explained my situation to the secretary, and she agreed to help. She spoke passable English, and as we drove through Munich, she said that her friend had been "an executioner before Hitler, during Hitler, and after Hitler," but she did not know where he now lived. I inwardly groaned, but knew with the bomb devastation in Munich, a permanent residence for anyone was almost impossible. Many people lived in cellars and in the remnants of buildings; often several families shared a single cellar, and many moved from building to building. As bulldozers cleared more rubble from the streets, new cellars and buildings became usable, and the population was in constant flux.

She suggested that we try his old building; I agreed and resigned myself to a long search. While I followed her directions, which had to be corrected several times to skirt rubble filled streets, she told me that her husband had been killed in North Africa and that the Gestapo had taken away most of her family and friends. She had been spared, but she was alone. I looked at her, estimated her age to be around thirty and realized that the entirety of her adult life had been spent in tyranny and war. I had no conception of what that could have been like, and, although I desperately wanted to, I couldn't think of anyway to make her feel better.

Fortunately, we located her friend's building which broke our awkward reveries. I waited with the jeep while she spoke to some people who lived there. She returned and told me that her friend had moved to a building in another section of Munich. She again directed me, and by the time we located the proper building dusk was settling, and I was anxious both to finish the job and to return to the safety of headquarters. A soldier out at night was sometimes a target for snipers.

The building was a low apartment house and appeared to be intact, something of a rarity in Munich. We found her friend's door on the second floor, and after repeated knocking it was opened by an older man with a sad face and a soft voice. The two friends exchange amenities, and we were invited into his room. They conversed some more; I don't know what was said, but both seemed delighted to see each other. Apparently, my purpose was explained, because he informed me that his family had performed executions for 200 years, and he wanted the job. He offered me a chair and a thin slice of black bread as we discussed the arrangements of transportation and passes. He told me that I shouldn't worry; he knew what to do.

With the second hangman secured, I traveled to Landsberg to meet Sergeant John Woods. Landsberg is not far from Munich, but it was a much smaller and older town. Many of its buildings dated to the fourteenth century, and the prison was housed in an old fortress that was built in the shape of a cross, a common design. The prison had been used as a concentration camp at the start of the war; now one wing was used for Nazi war criminals, and the other wings held civilian criminals. Landsberg later became a subsidy camp of Dachau

41

and was known as Lager #3. The inmates were used for forced labor, as were most inmates in the subsidy camps, and it was comprised of several barracks surrounded by an electrified fence. At the end of the war its operators were ordered to dispose of any evidence of the camp. They accomplished this by burning the barracks with the prisoners inside. Any prisoners escaping the flames were shot. The allied army found only twisted, charred bodies that had been fused by fire.

At Landsberg, I contacted First Lieutenant Holguin of the 47th Infantry Anti-Tank Company which was headquartered in a brick building that had been the office and home of the German town major. By any standards the quarters were comfortable and were complete with a garden and fountain and a German couple who maintained the grounds and rooms.

After I stowed my gear and ate lunch, Lieutenant Holguin escorted me to the prison, which was a short distance from the company headquarters, and to the main courtyard where Woods was working on the second gallows.

I had been warned that Woods was an unpredictable trouble maker with a violent temper. I found none of these descriptions to be true. In the time that we worked together Woods was professional and knowledgeable in a difficult occupation. He was respectful, friendly, and controlled when on duty. He did have a predilection for beer, and was given to verbal and physical outbursts when he was drunk. He freely expressed his hatred of Germans; a hatred rooted in the fact that he had lost several friends at the Malmedy Massacre, which occurred in Belgium when 190 American P.O.W.'s were herded into a field, stripped and machine gunned to death. He fraternized just as freely with German women, an apparent contradiction that was shared by most soldiers.

Woods was a short, stocky Texan of Irish descent who was a career soldier. He was secretive about his personal life, because as he put it, "not everyone likes what I do for a living." He never discussed his family; he once stated that his home town was San Antonio, but retracted that on a later occasion. In one beer-fueled conversation he told me that his neighbor had been a hangman at a Texas prison, but he refused to name the prison. When Woods was a teenager his neighbor invited him to watch a hanging. Woods accepted, saw several more, and subsequently because his neighbor's assistant. He was a hangman when he joined the army, and although he was a combat soldier who had seen action in North Africa and Normandy, he had served as an executioner for the army for over twenty years.

Woods was stretching his ropes with a duffel bag filled with sand. After introductions he stowed his ropes and volunteered to show me around. The courtyard, where we stood, was large enough to have several linden and chestnut shade trees and a greenhouse. It was completely enclosed by a wall, two prison cell blocks, and a corridor between the blocks. There were two entrances to the courtyard: one in the center of the corridor, and one in the rear of the wall which led to the cemetery. The two gallows stood on either side of the corridor entrance. Both gallows were black with a heavy, black curtain covering the area where the body would drop. It was planned that the condemned would be escorted through the corridor entrance and led to alternate gallows. As one man dangled behind the curtain, another would be led up the stairs of the other gallows. Twenty-eight crude, black coffins waited in the cemetery to receive the bodies. Holguin explained that any body not immediately claimed by the next of kin would be buried in an unmarked grave within minutes of being cut down.

The tour was short, and at its end Woods announced that he had a date and needed to clean up. We shook hands, and I marveled that he could think of socializing amid his ghoulish preparations.

Holguin then introduced me to PFC Brain who was our interpreter from army intelligence. I gave him a copy of the death order that Colonel Fogarty had given to me. It was to be read in English and German to each of the condemned at least twenty-four hours before his execution; Brain needed to translate it into German. I reminded him that the hangings were scheduled for the day after tomorrow. He told me he'd be done in a few hours.

Brain was as good as his word, and after dinner, Holguin, Brain, and I entered the cell block. I was to read the order, which ended with the phrase, "by the neck until dead," in English; Brain would read the translation.

As Holguin opened the doors to the cell block, I was nervous, maybe even scared. I wasn't frightened for my safety, the men were behind bars, but fearful of the type of men that I'd see. These were men that had killed and tortured thousands of human beings apparently without thought or remorse. Images of melodramatic movie villains, deranged monsters, and the devil himself flashed through my mind.

None of my imagined images matched what I saw. Without exception, the most accurate description for each of the twenty-eight men was average. There were no towering giants, no fierce expressions, no malevolent smirks. Several were middle aged men with slight builds, thinning hair and sagging faces. None would have stood out in a crowd. Perhaps their uniforms with SS regalia made them more imposing, but in their baggy prison denims, they more resembled tired factory workers than infidels.

The three of us proceeded from cell to cell. Each prisoner was required to stand, state his name for the record, and listen to the death order. Each complied without emotion; the men already knew their fates. Only one, Martin Weiss, who was the last commandant of Dachau, stated in English, "It is not necessary to read it again. I understand English very well." Weiss pulled impatiently on his goatee when Brain read the order in German anyway.

The following day the German hangman and his assistants arrived, and he and Woods spent several hours testing the gallows. I spent several hours in a meeting led by Colonel Thurston, a regimental Commander from Regensberg, who outlined the procedures that each person would follow the next day.

Early on May 28th, which was an exceptionally nice spring day, the executions began under the direction of Colonel Thurston. Each of the condemned was escorted from his cell by four MP guards and two officers to the corridor entrance between the gallows. The officers led, and when they appeared in the doorway, Colonel Thurston gave the command to attention. The officers proceeded to the top of the steps that descended to the courtyard, and the condemned stood between them. The colonel then read the death order to the assemblage.

The assemblage included two officers, Holguin and myself, Brain, two army chaplains, Peter Rush, a Catholic, and Karl Almer, a Lutheran, and the German prison chaplain, all of whom were at the base of the steps and would escort the condemned to one of the gallows. In the courtyard there were two army doctors, a former captain from the legal branch of the army who was the United States' legal witness, two army reporters, an army photographer and his assistant. The mayor of Munich served as the German witness and several MP's ringed the yard. Two prison inmates waited with carts by the cemetery gate to receive the bodies. No civilian reporters were allowed, and although the executions were not kept secret, they received little publicity. Stars and Stripes carried a single article and photograph; wire services used that article to inform their papers.

(I had passed my camera to the photographer's assistant and asked him to take pictures for me. He obliged and stood directly behind his boss to capture the same images. These pictures are seen for the first time in this book.)

I was a bundle of nerves and emotions as I waited at my post at the bottom of the stairs. I could see Woods and the German on the gallows with hoods and ropes, and I knew that the men were going to die. Not tomorrow, not the next day, but right now. I'd never seen a man die, and I didn't know if I could take it. However, I desperately wanted to be able to take it. I didn't want to appear squeamish or weak to my fellow officers. I knew that this was an important event for the army, and I didn't want to be the cause to any problems or mishaps.

Friederich Wilhelm Rupert, who beat prisoners with a riding crop and arranged the gassing of 90 Russian officers, was the first prisoner that we escorted to the gallows. I stared at the ground, concentrated on putting one foot in front of the other, and I wildly hoped that I was staying with the rest of the group. On the gallows, Rupert spoke his last words, "Tell my wife that I was thinking of her and I died bravely." Woods placed the hood over his head, fitted the rope, and tied his arms and legs with army web belts to prevent flailing. Woods sprung the hatch, and Rupert dropped behind the curtain; the rope groaned and swayed. I shut my eyes and thought, "My God, how can I be doing this?"

Fortunately for me I wasn't allowed time to reflect. I had to return to my post at the bottom of the stairs to escort the second condemned man, Anton Anders who assisted in the freezing experiments, to the other gallows. Dr. Sigmund Rasher, the true architect of the freezing experiments, escaped Allied judgment. On Himmler's orders he was shot at Dachau in 1944 for giving false information to his superiors. The colonel again read the order, we walked him to the gallows, the hatch opened, and the rope groaned. By this time the army doctors had declared Rupert dead, he had been removed from the noose, and his body was being wheeled to the cemetery.

Hanging does not immediately kill a man; however, in a proper hanging he loses all consciousness and feeling the moment the large coils of the noose snap his neck. At that point his brain is disconnected from his body and his respiration stops. Complete cession of his heart beat, the official determination of death, occurs within eight to twelve minutes after he drops. During that time he does not gasp or choke; he may have bitten off his tongue and lost control of his bowels when his neck snapped, but he would not be aware of either.

We followed the procedure described above for about two and a half hours until we walked to the prison for a lunch break. I had no appetite; I picked at the food on my tray, smoked, which made my mouth dry, and sipped coffee, which made my stomach sour. As an example of how a person can become acclimated to a situation, I ate a full meal that evening, and the following day I had no problem finishing my lunch. By the time we hung the last group of seven men on May 29th, their final walks, the hoods, the thunks of the falling bodies, the groaning ropes, and the black coffins were all familiar and routine.

I wondered about this change in myself and considered if any of the thousands of concentration camp prisoners had come to regard their situation as routine. I then wondered if the SS guards had thought of their acts of torture and killing as part of a normal day. I did not want to believe that mass death, piles of twisted bodies, and the deliberate attempt to exterminate a group of people could be considered routine or normal by anyone. I wondered if the guards discussed their work on their off duty hours and compared the numbers of prisoners they had beaten and killed during the day. Did they show off their trophies made of human skin? Did they brag, as Simon Kiern did, that they could kill a man with one blow? And then did they write love letters to their wives and girl friends and pass around pictures of their children. The idea that the guards could have thought what they were doing was normal chilled me.

Yet, was I any different from them? In forty-eight hours the task of escorting men to their deaths had become routine for me, and I would talk about, although not brag as some may have, about my experience. The men that we hung were as dead as any concentration camp victim; were we of the same character as the SS guards? I decided that we were not; the men hung at Landsberg had been tried. Their crimes were such that they received the death penalty, and the tribunals were not blood thirsty; most war criminals received prison terms or were acquitted for lack of evidence. We could not be considered the same as the criminals that we hung who were indiscriminate and brutal in their actions.

The fact that I became accustomed to hangings rather quickly still nagged at me. Had I been a German SS guard would I have followed the cruel practices of my comrades? Would I have been able to starve people, beat them, hang them, burn them? Would I have been pleased with the number of prisoners that I killed? Would I brag about my abilities to torture people? I could not answer these questions because I was not raised in a society that promoted such activities. Americans were not angels and had in many situations exhibited cruel and improper behavior to their enemies. However, this type of behavior was not condoned or promoted by the government, and it certainly did not become acceptable to society. Nonetheless, at the end of those two days, I had a better understanding of how the Nazis were able to perpetrate their horrendous activities.

Otto Forschner was the third man to hang. His age was recorded at 44, but he looked closer to 60 or 65. Despite the warm day, he wore a full length black overcoat. Before he dropped he said, "I forgive the court for passing sentence on me, and I thank the Americans for treating me so well in prison."

Martin Gottfried Weiss, commandant of Dachau from 1942 to 1943, was the fourth to drop. He had no last words, but he had hoped for a reprieve based on statements that he had done all that he could for the prisoners. The reprieve was not granted.

Egelbert Valentin Niedermyer had been the administrator of the crematorium. He died silently, and was pronounced dead nine minutes after he dropped. He died in the shortest amount of time.

Dr. Karl Klaus Schilling was 74 and the oldest criminal to hang. He was unsteady when we escorted him across the courtyard, and he needed assistance to climb the steps of the gallows. He managed to stand erect on the platform as the rope went under his pointed goatee. His last words were, "Schnell, bitte, schnell." (Hurry, please hurry.) At his trial he had asked to be allowed to live to complete his malaria experiments despite the fact that those experiments had killed over 400 people, most of whom were Polish priests.

Joseph Seuss, who bound prisoners' arms behind them and strung them up by their wrists showed some remorse with his last words. He started, "I only hope Germany will be strong..." After a moments reflection he said, "No. No. I mean I hope Germany will be beautiful again."

Simon Kiern, a block leader with a penchant for beating prisoners and using them for target practice, had no remorse. He clasped a bouquet of flowers that his wife had given to him the day before. He said, "Those who take my life will have to answer to God for it." He also asked that his wife be told that, "he would be waiting for her in heaven." When I heard those words I thought what a monumental ego he must have to believe that he would be allowed in heaven.

Willi Frey, who was only twenty-three, had boasted in his cell that "I will go to the gallows singing Give Me Five Minutes More and Open the Door, Richard." It was reported that in the courtyard he whispered, "I am dying like Jesus on the cross...without fault," although I never heard that. He did not sing.

Christof Knoll was an habitual criminal who had been a pre war prisoner at Dachau. When the SS guards noticed his natural brutality, he was made a trustee and encouraged to beat prisoners to death. He died silently. Franz Trenkle, who beat prisoners after placing them in a prone position on a table or desk, dropped without a word. The following men also died silently: Emil Kohl, Fritz Bechey, Alex Bernard, Hans Pickowski, Rudolf Stuttrop, Franz Boettger, Johann Georg Kick, Willy Temple, Victor Kirsch, Otto Moll, John Eicheladorf, Michael Redwitz, Wilhelm Welter, Fritz Hintermeir, Paul Walter, and Anton Endress.

The last man to hang was Leonard Anselm Eichberger, who had committed acts of cruelty to individual prisoners. He had one leg, and because it was feared that he might use his crutch as a weapon, it was originally planned that he would be carried to the gallows. He begged to be able to walk his last steps under his own power. Colonel Thurston acquiesced, and Eichberger clumped up the gallows steps and balanced himself on his single leg until the trap door opened.

CHAPTER SIX

Regular Duties

After the Landsberg executions I returned to Munich and was again assigned the duty of registering vehicles. I had comfortable quarters in an apartment building that the army had taken over to house its officers. Our headquarters had a popular officers club, and I spent a good deal of my free time drinking and socializing with my fellow officers. When we had free weekends, several of us drove to Chiemsee Lake, which is about forty miles southeast of Munich. We rented a row boat from two peasant women who lived in a hut along with their goats and chickens. They charged us two marks, or twenty cents in American currency for the day. Despite what I thought was a ridiculously low rate, the women were always happy to see us and took pains to wipe the seats of the boat.

Before the war Munich had been a modern metropolis with high rise apartment and office buildings, wide streets, a transit system, and a busy commerce district. Much of this had been destroyed by the war, but I saw signs of repair and reconstruction. With the help of the army, most of the streets had been cleared of rubble, and the city managed to get some of the street cars in operation. The citizens responded to the appearance of the street cars with enthusiasm that bordered on hysteria. Crowds of people, far more than the cars could hold, attempted to board at each stop. People hung on the sides of the cars, ran along side them, pulled other passengers off, and pushed, shoved, and fought to get a place on the cars. This behavior, which was out of character for the normally reserved

Germans, continued until there was enough cars running to accommodate the passengers.

Another event also resulted in a massive crowd, although one that exercised complete control. On a Spring afternoon three priests, each holding a pole of a tri-pole apparatus that held a huge religious banner, led a procession thought the main streets of Munich. Munich was the most Catholic of all German cities, and, before Hitler, such processions were common. Hitler banned such celebrations of faith in the thirties and sent many priests to concentration camps, over ten thousand were sent to Dachau alone. The Germans now reveled in the opportunity to express their religious beliefs, and by the time the procession passed our headquarters, I thought that all of Munich was participating. About a block past our building, the procession stopped. One priest handed his pole to his companion, stepped off the street and into the ruins of a building to relieve himself. The entire procession, hundreds of people, waited patiently while the priest answered his call of nature. This patience of the people was in sharp contrast, their impatience and aggressive behavior when boarding street cars.

A few days after the procession, I was nearly shot. A private and I were driving through the city on a routine errand. As we passed through a section of bombed out buildings a bullet shattered out windshield. Reflexively, I recoiled and ducked my head, and a second bullet whined passed my ear. The private missed being killed only because of his habit of hunching over the steering wheel when he drove. A third bullet grazed the hump of his shoulder blades and passed through the back of the seat. I screamed at him to stop, which he was already doing, and we dove for cover behind the jeep. I pulled my pistol from its holster, for the first time not on the target range, and looked wildly around. The sniper had stopped shooting, but both the private and I were certain that he had fired from a building on our right. Not allowing myself to think, I announced that we were going after him. We dashed to the building, entered, and faced piles of rubble. Carefully, I was thinking more now and realized our danger, we picked out way among the piles, but found no one. We searched a couple of more buildings with the same result, and I knew the attacker was long gone.

Unfortunately, this was not an isolated incident. While most of the Germans accepted our presence and cooperated with us, some did not, and American soldiers were subjected to sniper fire and other random violence. Some soldiers had been killed by these acts, and the private and I were lucky to have emerged unscathed.

The private thought that we had been attached by a Werewolf, SS soldiers who Hitler claimed would never surrender and continue to fight from the Bavarian forests, and he told this version to his buddies at headquarters, each time embellishing the events a little more in his favor. I had been in Germany long enough to know that if the Werewolves did exist they were not organized, and our sniper was more likely a disgruntled individual who, for whatever reason, refused to accept that Germany had lost the war. Such individuals couldn't make a difference in Germany's occupation or reconstruction, but could create danger and death for vulnerable soldiers, as the private and I had been that afternoon. Peace, I was reminded, is a difficult process.

CHAPTER SEVEN

Preparation for Nuremberg

In July, 1946, I was transferred to the Provost Marshal Section Third Army in Heidelberg and again given the duty of registering vehicles. However, before I got my quarters squared away, I was ordered to Augsburg with Lieutenant Colonel McLaughlin ostensibly for an inspection tour. This was the army's way of giving us a week's leave, and we took advantage of it. After checking in to headquarters at Augsburg, we each went our separate ways to conduct our "inspections." I visited Zugspitz, which was near the Crow's Nest, Hitler's mountain retreat where, I learned, he had applied his meager artistic talents to painting.

When I returned from leave, Colonel Philip Clayton sent word that I was to see him in his office. I was nervous, Colonel Clayton was a full Colonel and the Third Army Provost Marshal; he didn't send for second lieutenants unless they were in trouble.

Colonel Clayton put me at ease, offered me a cigarette, and congratulated me on my fine work at Landsberg. He then told me that he had information that the Nuremberg trials would soon be coming to a close and that several death sentences were expected. Since I had had experience at Landsberg, the colonel thought I would be the person to coordinate the arrangements for Nuremberg. He looked at me carefully and said that because of the nature of the duty he could only request, not order me, but he hoped that I would accept. He offered me an irresistible plum; upon completion of the executions I would immediately be transferred state side and discharged.

In the time it took me to crush out my cigarette, several thoughts zoomed through my mind. I was relieved that I was not in trouble, but displeased that I would again be involved with ropes, hoods, and falling bodies. I realized that my week's leave had been arranged to put me in a favorable mood and to make me beholden. I figured that if I refused the colonel I wouldn't spend the rest of my tour on such light duty as vehicle registration and I wouldn't be going home anytime soon. I accepted and thanked the Colonel for the opportunity to be of assistance.

Colonel Clayton had anticipated me, and he pulled a folder from his desk drawer and briefed me. He told me that unlike Landsberg and any of the hundreds of other executions throughout Germany, those at Nuremberg were politically charged. The defendants were the highest leaders of the Nazi machine, not anonymous SS guards at a concentration camp. These men formulated the policies and philosophy of the nation; Goering was Reichmarshall and second only to Hitler. Hundreds of reporters were covering the trial, and the world was waiting for the verdicts. Several groups hoped that the trials would verify their goals. The Allies wanted to prove the guilt of the defendants, and to have their punishment serve as a deterrent against future atrocities. Nazi supporters thought the evidence would vindicate the defendants and the party; others wanted to demonstrate that the Allies had been as ruthless and blood thirsty as the Germans. The colonel said that he had information from army intelligence that protests from German citizens and from a nearby P.O.W. camps were expected if the trial resulted in death sentences, as it surely would.

Because of these factors, Colonel Clayton explained, everything about the executions and their preparations, including that very briefing, were classified as top secret. I would, on paper, still be assigned to vehicle registration at Heidelberg, but I would coordinate the construction of the gallows at Landsberg and their transport to Nuremberg. I would have no written orders defining my position; however, word would be passed to all supply and transport depots that they must fill any of my requests immediately. I was to tell no one of my responsibilities or give any reasons for my requisitions.

Three gallows, the colonel continued, would be made at Landsberg prison and moved to Nuremberg at a later date. This necessitated some special construction that allowed for the easy dismantling, transportation, and reconstruction of the gallows. The Colonel estimated that four to five weeks would be needed to make such gallows and that Sergeant John Woods would supervise their construction. Five M.P.'s, specially selected by their commanding officers, would assist Woods. The colonel told me that I would meet the men in his office the following morning before they drove to Landsberg. He advised me to arrange for my registration duties to be covered, requisition a plane from the Air Corps Wing in Heidelberg and fly to Landsberg as soon as possible.

I was dazed when I left Colonel Clayton's office. I had been put in charge of preparations for the most important executions of the century. The entire world was waiting for them. If anything went wrong, I knew where the blame would fall. I didn't sleep well that night.

The next morning I met the five M.P.'s in Colonel Clayton's office. The Colonel was not present, and the men looked at me with anticipation. I wasn't prepared to lead a briefing, but I inquired about the background of each of the men, described their duties, stressed the importance of their tasks, and the necessity of their cooperation. One man, PFC Malta, the self appointed spokesman of the group, told me not to worry; they could handle the job with no problems.

The men left for Landsberg, which is about 175 miles from Heidelberg, in the two jeeps that had been requisitioned for their use. I closed out some work in my office, and that afternoon I took Colonel Clayton's advice and requisitioned myself a plane for my trip to Landsberg.

As I dialed the air strip I figured my chance of getting a plane was about zero. The Army Air Corps had a few small planes that were used to transport the top brass around Germany. Second Lieutenants rode in jeeps and trucks. However, by simply supplying my name to the duty officer, I was told a plane and a pilot would be ready for my use tomorrow morning. I was impressed with my new power, and I was more impressed the next morning when a plane and a pilot were actually waiting for me at the air strip.

The plane was a L-4, a small plane with two seats, and overhead wing, and a noisy engine and had mostly been used for observation during the war. My pilot was First Lieutenant Buck, a husky man with a good natured grin. At his request, Buck more or less became my personal pilot. He liked to fly and get away from the air strip. He never inquired about the nature of my trips, and he busied himself while on the ground at Landsberg. I suspected that he saw a girlfriend, but I never asked.

I was petrified as Buck strapped me into the passenger seat. I had never flown in this type of plane before, and it looked old and rickety and very much like those planes that I had seen crash so many times in the newsreels at the movies. Buck slapped my shoulder and told me we'd be in Landsberg before I knew it. He hopped into the pilot's seat and started the engine; I gritted my teeth and prayed. Once air borne, I decided that flying wasn't that bad, and I looked over the side at the German landscape. It was a clear day, and the view enthralled me. By the time we landed and hour or so later, I enjoyed flying and was looking forward to the return trip.

I was quartered at the 47th Anti-Tank Company where I had stayed during the executions in May; Lieutenant Holguin still commanded the unit. After we stowed our gear, Holguin escorted me to the prison work shop; Buck found his own amusements. I would have liked to share the project with Buck, but its secrecy was paramount. The only people who knew what was being built in the workshop were Colonel Clayton, Holguin,

Woods, the five M.P.'s, and myself. The workshop was restricted for our use; even the other members of the Anti-Tank Company were not aware of the project. The workshop was large, and, despite the summer weather, it was cold. Two coal stoves burned at either end, but they had a limited effect. Woods was perched on a stool and supervising three German prisoners that were cutting wood with a band saw. When he saw us, he stopped the saw and told the Germans to wait. He motioned us to a work bench out of their earshot. Apparently, Woods had received a briefing about secrecy at Third Army Headquarters.

We exchanged greetings, and he reported that the work was progressing well.

"How long do you think it will take?" I asked.

"I figure about eight to ten days for each gallows. Twenty-five
to thirty days total," Woods said. "It's the drilling and bolting them together that takes the time."

"Will you have them ready by October?"

"We should. We'll work longer shifts if we hit a problem. I have, by the way, made a slight alteration in the design." He picked a device that resembled an elaborate door latch. "In May one of the trap doors swung back up and hit the guy in the face as he dropped. I've never seen it happen before, but it broke the guy's jaw and teeth and bloodied him up pretty good. I'm not going to let that happen again, and this latch will hold the trap door open until I release it. No one else will get hit like that."

Both Holguin and I expressed our admiration, and Woods beamed. I knew he was capable of performing his duty without my supervision, and I prepared to leave. I asked him what materials he needed.

"We got plenty of lumber for now, sir, but we need some paint."

"Fine. Do you want black?"

"I'm not sure, sir. Trucking black lumber all the way to Nuremberg might look funny, and somebody could figure out

58

what we're carrying. I thought olive drab might be a better color. Nobody's going to think much about trucks carrying olive drab lumber. I think that color would be better."

I agreed and told him I'd get some for him as soon as I could.

"I figure we'll need about twenty-five gallons", Woods said.

If Woods had asked for twenty-five pounds of gold, it would have been an easier request. The army painted everything olive drab, and now that the war was over, everything was getting a new coat of paint. Olive drab was being used in the thousands of gallons by every unit in Europe.

Back in Heidelberg I started calling quartermaster depots. After several hours, located a fifty gallon drum of paint at a depot to the east. The depot had ordered the paint for its own use and had waited weeks for it to arrive. I told the quartermaster that I needed twenty-five gallons, and I gave my name. He reluctantly parted with his booty. I called our motor pool and requisitioned a truck to pick up the paint, and one was immediately dispatched. I called Lieutenant Buck and inquired about the feasibility of flying the paint the Landsberg. He said that the L-4 couldn't take off with two people and the paint; two planes would be necessary. He suggested that the paint be put into five gallon cans for better weight distribution. To his credit, he never asked why I needed so much paint. Through the duty officer at the Air Corps, I requisitioned two planes, an L-4 and an L-5, and arranged for our supply depot to pour the paint into five gallon cans. I accomplished all of this in a single afternoon without filling out one piece of paperwork and with no delays. I simply gave my name. Power is a heady thing.

During the final weeks of the summer I made several trips to Landsberg. Most were made by air, although I drove my jeep a couple of times, and Lieutenant Buck was always happy to fly me. Under Woods' supervision the work on the gallows was on schedule and my roll had become that of a glorified gopher. My presence at Landsberg wasn't especially necessary, but I enjoyed the trips and I enjoyed socializing with Woods, Holguin, and Buck. I invented excuses to stay in Landsberg over weekends. Holguin had access to a sail boat on Amersee Lake just outside the city. The boat had belonged to Landsberg's mayor, and when the army took the mayor's house for its headquarters, the boat was included. I spent several afternoon on the boat, swimming, fishing, drinking beer, and enjoying the company of friends.

A call from Colonel Clayton on September 10, 1946, brought me back to the reality of my duty. He informed me that on September 12th, a single war criminal would be hung at Landsberg Prison and that I would be the officer in charge. He told me that I was chosen because I was experienced and could make the arrangements quickly. I looked at my watch; even if I could get a plane immediately, I wouldn't arrive at Landsberg until late afternoon. I didn't see how I could possibly have everything ready in a day's time.

I shouldn't have worried. Lieutenant Holguin had been alerted to the situation. He met me at the air strip and said that he had the death order in his office and that PFC Brain was working on the German translation. The death order had to be read to the accused twenty-four hours before the execution, in this case, by 0800 hours the next morning. Holguin assured me that Brain would be ready well before that dead line.

That evening Holguin told me what he knew about the accused. His name was Justus Gerstenberg, and he was an older man, too old for active service, but he belonged to Germany's Home Guard Forces. Gerstenberg had killed a wounded American paratrooper rather than take him prisoner. There were witnesses to the event, and after the war, he had been captured and tried at Landsberg. His trial lasted several days, a long time in comparison to most tribunal trials. He was found guilty and sentenced to death.

I was in Holguin's office by dawn the next morning. Brain was already there with his completed translation of the death order. The three of us walked to the prison to perform our duty.

Gerstenberg stood as we entered his cell. He was a small man with thick, black hair that had grown long and unruly. His face was deeply lined and expressionless; his eyes looked at us, but didn't seem to focus. His only response was a single nod when asked if he understood the order. He sat down before we left the cell.

I wondered if Gerstenberg did understand what he had done wrong. Through the Home Guard he had been charged with protecting his village. The American, although he was wounded, was the enemy, and Gerstenberg probably thought he was doing his duty when he killed him. I wondered if I would have reacted differently if the German U-boats had disembarked men on the New Jersey shore. I realized that I had voided Woods' cardinal rule about hanging: never think about the man's guilt or innocence. That was for the court to decide.

In the courtyard Woods was stretching his ropes on the gallows that he had used in May. I noticed that PFC Malta was assisting him. We waved at them and returned to headquarters for breakfast.

On September 12th, at 0700 Holguin, Brain, Woods, Malta, an army doctor, the prison chaplain, two prison guards, an officer from the Provost Marshal Section, and myself met in the prison courtyard. I decided that Brain, the two guards, the chaplain, and I would escort Gerstenberg to the gallows. Holguin, the doctor, and the Provost Marshal officer would wait at the steps of the gallows, and Woods and Malta would be on the platform. Unlike the executions in May, there were no civilian witnesses and no reporters or photographers from Stars and Stripes or any other newspaper. (The pictures of the hanging were taken with my camera by Holguin and are seen for the first time in this book.)

At 0730, Brain and I entered Gerstenberg's cell and again read the death order. I noticed that he had neatly made his bunk, but he had left his breakfast untouched on its tray. When Brain finished reading the translation, Gerstenberg leaned forward and whispered something to him. Brain told me that he wanted to spend time with the chaplain again. I agreed, and we waited outside while the chaplain comforted him.

The walk across the courtyard took only a few moments, but they were tense moments. Gerstenberg's face was still expressionless, and he fixed his eyes straight ahead. He carefully matched his steps to ours. I realized that I was again leading a man to his death.

At the gallows steps Brain joined Holguin and the doctor; I accompanied Gerstenberg to the platform. This was the first and only time that I stood on the platform during a hanging. The Provost Marshal Officer read the death order for a final time, and Malta tied Gerstenberg's hands and feet with army web belts. Brain asked if he had any last words. Gerstenberg looked at us and said, "Nein." Woods applied the hood and adjusted the noose. At 0800 he released the trap door. From my position I could see his body drop. The rope became taut, and the coils snapped his head forward. His body convulsed for a few seconds then swayed as lifelessly as a sand filled duffel bag. I noticed that the trap door was firmly anchored, and for some reason, I was inordinately pleased that Woods' new latch had worked. Some minutes later the doctor pronounced Justus Gerstenberg dead.

CHAPTER EIGHT

Nuremberg

Nuremberg was settled in the eleventh century, and during the Renaissance it became an economic and cultural center. Much of its medieval art and architecture, including ancient stone watch towers and bridges, was preserved, and these became tourist attractions for the city.

In the 1930's the city had a new attraction ¾ Nazis, and they made Nuremberg their spiritual home. Its landmarks and gingerbread houses with red title roofs and carved dormers appealed to Hitler. Nuremberg became the site of the annual Parteitajen, week long rallies devoted to glorifying Hitler and Nazism. Albert Speer arranged the rallies that began with church bells announcing Hitler's arrival and ending with a climatic march of a quarter million torch bearing party members to Zeppelin Field where they proclaimed their support and adulation for Hitler with frenzied shouts and cheers.

By the end of the war Nuremberg was declared, "among the dead cities of the European Continent." It had been bombed in Allied raids eleven times with as many as 10,000 bombs dropped in a single raid. The city was ninety-one per cent destroyed, and it lacked electricity, water, transportation, telephone, and a government. Its historic landmarks and quaint buildings lay in rubble. Some 30,000 bodies were buried under that rubble which gave the city a putrid stench; a massive population of rats threatened to overrun the few remaining survivors.

Amid the rubble a medieval fortress known as the Justizgebaube (Palace of Justice) remained intact. It had been hit by bombs five times, but it had weathered each blow. At the end of the war it was being used to house American soldiers. On its third floor was Room 600, a huge and, at one time, ornate hall, that had ample room for judges, defendants, lawyers and spectators. A prison consisting of four wings that radiated like spokes of a wheel was at the rear of the Palace. The prison was being used to house common criminals, but one wing could be made suitable for the war criminals. Within walking distance the battered, but still intact Grand Hotel afforded quarters for the judges, lawyers, and staff. The Tribunal decided that Nuremberg would be the site of the trial.

When the selection of Nuremberg was announced much speculation was made of the apparent irony. The Nazis would meet their ignominious ends in the city that had given them vitality. While that irony is appropriate, it was not a consideration. Facilities were needed for the trial, and by the sheer coincidence of bombing raids and patterns, Nuremberg was the only city in Germany with those facilities.

The trial of the war criminals was truly the trial of the century. By the time it started on November 20, 1945, it had overcome legal, logistical, and physical obstacles and had acquired the distinction of being "the first" in several areas.

The physical obstacles were daunting. With the exception of the Palace, the prison, and the Grand Hotel, Nuremberg was rubble. Streets were impassable and dwellings were non-existent. Facilities such as cafeterias, laundries, pharmacies, hospitals, and stores that were necessary to support a staff of workers did not exist.

The army, along with the labor supplied by 15,000

German P.O.W.'s and German women, cleared the streets. Gallons of disinfectant were used to mask the stench of rotting bodies. Under the direction of Captain Daniel Kiley, the Palace was repaired and remodeled to accommodate the bureaucracy necessary to house and try the criminals. A wing of the prison was prepared for the criminals, and the 6850th Internal Security Detachment (ISD) under the command of Colonel Burton Andrus was charged with keeping the prisoners alive and healthy for trial.

In May 1945, President Truman appointed Supreme Court Justice Robert Jackson to be the United States representative and chief prosecutor. Jackson became the main force behind the trial; he scouted the location, negotiated political differences among the Tribunal members, discussed and decided points of law, organized the prosecution team, and determined the court's methods and philosophy.

The trial was the first serious attempt to bring justice to war criminals. A feeble attempt was made by the Allies at the end of World War I. Of the nearly 5,000 possible criminals, twelve were brought to trial. Three of those never bothered to appear; charges were dismissed against three others; six received ridiculously light sentences. Jackson was determined not to repeat that fiasco, but he had little power on his side. The defendants would be judged by an International Tribunal made up of one representative from each allied nation--four total. This composition was without precedent--another first. The defendants would be tried by international law which had no provisions against the actions of the defendants. The Tribunal and the lawyers for the prosecution represented both Anglo-Saxon law and Continental law which did not have compatible philosophies. Continental law had no concept of criminal conspiracy, of which most of the defendants were guilty. The trial also had to be held in the languages of the Allies, English, French, and Russian, and the language of the defendants,

German. Jackson feared that translating and reading each document and the testimony of each witness four times would make the trial interminable.

Negotiations, insight, and ingenuity eventual removed most obstacles. The court became a hybrid of Anglo-Saxon and Continental law. The use of multiple judges reflected a Continental philosophy; opposing lawyers was an Anglo-Saxon contribution. IBM developed equipment that was able to broadcast simultaneous translations through a system of headphones. The equipment was the first of its kind, and its first use was at the Nuremberg trial. Colonel Murray Bernays of the War Department developed a theory of prosecution. He suggested that if the Nazi regime and its component parts such as the Gestapo and the SS were declared a criminal conspiracy then any members of the regime or its parts were criminals. The prosecution would only need to prove that a defendant was a member of one of the offending organizations to be guilty. Jackson thought the idea was brilliant and would allow for the effective prosecution of the Nazi leaders who, after all, did not actually slaughter people in concentration camps. The theory, though, would permit prosecution by ex post facto law; that is, belonging to the Nazi regime was declared criminal after the defendants joined. This was not proper law in either the Anglo-Saxon or the Continental philosophy. Nonetheless, the theory appealed to Jackson, and he argued that since the Nazis had violated numerous treaties they had to know that their regime was criminal. The argument was weak, but it became the basis for the prosecution.

Jackson feared two legal defenses. The first was that the defendants were following orders from a higher official; for most of the defendants this official was Hitler, who could not be prosecuted. The second was the Tu quo qu or "so did you," defense. The Nazis were being tried for waging an aggressive war; the Allies, most notably the Soviets, had likewise been aggressive. The Allies were also guilty of barbarous acts against civilians and P.O.W.'s, but not nearly to the extent of the Germans. After considerable negotiations the Tribunal decided that the defendants would simply not be allowed either avenue of defense.

While Jackson wrangled with legal questions and the politics of forming a Tribunal and while the Palace of Justice was renovated, the war criminals took their cells in the prison wing immediately adjacent to the Palace. Colonel Burton Andrus had charge of the prison and the prisoners. He managed the prisoners' visitations, meals, mail, possessions, exercise, conversations, transport to the trial, and their complaints.

Andrus was a career military man, although his career had not been distinguished. During World War I he had commanded Fort Oglethorpe in Georgia which was an army prison for its rapists and murderers. This experience prepared him for Nuremberg.

Andrus' colleagues were surprised at his appointment as commandant. He had never been know as the brightest officer, but he was known for being a stickler for petty details and regulations. He wore a shellacked green helmet, even outside of combat and often inside buildings, and carried a riding crop, two affections he modeled from his idol, General George Patton. He had the reputation of a martinet, but a more accurate description would have been of a man who was wholly impressed by military pomp. One of his first acts as commandant was to design personally an insignia for his ISD soldiers. He truly hoped that Jackson would adopt this insignia for the Tribunal and its staff. He envisioned all the lawyers, judges, secretaries, custodians, cafeteria workers, and spectators displaying pins or patches of his design.

Whatever his shortcomings, Andrus proved an able

commandant. He thoroughly briefed his soldiers and added that any breach in discipline would result in a court martial. The prisoners were denied belts and shoelaces, and any sharp objects such as pens and eyeglasses were removed from their cells each evening. The cell block and stairs were strung with chicken wire to prevent any prisoner from hurling himself to his death. Guards were instructed to monitor each prisoner in his cell at intervals of no more than two minutes. When Robert Ley committed suicide, an act Andrus took personally, he ordered a continuous watch on each prisoner. A spot light shone into each cell at night, and each prisoner was required to have his hands in view to avoid any chance of unseen actions in shadows or under blankets.

On October 19, 1945, one month before the start of the trial, indictments were read to each of the prisoners. Each was charged with one or more of the following counts:
The acquiring of totalitarian control of Germany. Utilization of the Nazi control for foreign aggression.

Violation of international treaties, agreements, and aggression.

Murder and ill treatment of civilian populations. Deportation for slave labor. Killing of hostages.

Persecution of populations on political, racial, and religious grounds.

By late November 1945, the Palace of Justice was complete, the Tribunal was formed, the prosecution teams and the defense lawyers were ready, and the prisoners had been indicted. Daniel Kiley used 875 workers, over 5000 gallons of paint, a quarter million bricks, 100,000 board feet of lumber, and over a million feet of wire and cable to refurbish the Palace. During the trial 650 clerical workers were used to generate 50,000 typed pages, 4,000 recordings, and 30,000 photocopies.

The cafeteria served 1,500 lunches each court day, and the army processed and cleared 250 press representatives and 60,000 spectators.

Sir Geoffrey Lawrence of Great Britain was the principal judge of the Tribunal; Sir Norman Birkett was the British alternate. Francis Biddle was the United States' judge, and John Parker was the alternate. Henri Donnediu De Vahres and Robert Falco were the French judge and alternate. Ian Timofeevich Nikitchenko was the Soviet judge, and Alexander Volchkov was the alternate. Supreme Court Justice Robert Jackson headed the United States' prosecution team. Sir Hartly Showcross was the titular head of the British team, although Sir David Maxwell-Fyfe supervised the team. The Soviet team was headed by Lieutenant General Roman A. Rudenko. Lawyers had been assigned to each of the defendants, and the criminals awaited their fates. The trial of the century was ready to begin.

CHAPTER NINE

The Prisoners

Not every war criminal would meet his fate at Nuremberg. Some, like Goebbels, Himmler, and Hitler escaped judgment through suicide. Some escaped to South American countries and to the United States. Some of these, like Adolf Eichmann, were caught and tried later. Others, like Joseph Mengle, died before any earthly judgment could be rendered. Those on trial at Nuremberg consisted of some of the most powerful Nazis who were responsible for horrible policies and some who had only a peripheral connection to the party.

Hans Frank spent his life searching for respectability to impress his first and greatest love, Lilli Gau, the daughter of a Munich industrialist. Frank came from a poor family. His father was a womanizing lawyer of some disrepute; his mother had been a peasant. During his brief courtship of Lilli Gau, Frank's father was found guilty of embezzlement. Gau's father forbade Frank to ever see his daughter again.

Frank managed to receive a law degree, but with Germany's economy in shambles after World War I, he found little work. On a whim he defended a Nazi for free; he won the case and caught Hitler's eye. By 1939 he was the Minister of Justice, the top jurist in Germany; he owned five palatial homes and traveled in a chauffeured limousine.

Success came at a price. Frank was expected to bend the

Justus Gerstenberg awaiting execution September 12, 1946.

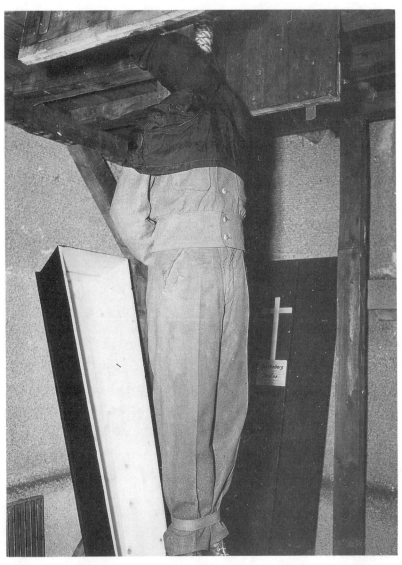

The body of Gerstenberg as it hangs awaiting for U.S. Army
declaration of death.

Author on extreme left as the U.S. Army photographer records
the execution.

PFC Malta holds the arm of the condemned, Sgt. Woods in the
background and author on the right.

Entrance to Dachau

Left to right: Interpreter, author, Lt. Holguin, Lt. Col. Smith and unknown Major.

The left gallows in the courtyard of Landsberg prison.

Witness awaiting an execution.

law to fit Hitler's demands. Frank sold his soul the first time in 1933 on the Night of the Long Knives or the Roehm Purge. Hitler had demanded the execution or Ernst Roehm and other Storm Troopers that had supposedly been disloyal to the party. Frank protested that they could not be executed without a trial. Hitler insisted, Frank capitulated and kept his position and property; Roehm and his followers were shot.

When Poland was defeated in 1939, Hitler named Frank Governor General and gave him supreme power in the region. He moved into Wawel Castle, the historic home of Polish royalty, called his wife the Queen of Poland, ruled and lived like a king, and sold his soul a second time. Frank's surname had been shortened from Frankfurter, he had Jewish ancestry, and he was not anti-Semitic. Nonetheless, when Hitler demanded that Poland be purged of Jews, Frank did so with enthusiasm. Over a million Jews were deported to Germany for slave labor, and thousands more died of starvation in Poland.

In 1943, Lilli Gau, his beloved, sought out Frank for assistance in locating a relative that had been lost at the Russian front. Frank began an affair with Gau and wished to divorce his wife and marry Lilli. Hitler, who did not allow divorce and was exceedingly prudish, refused to allow Frank to continue his relationship with Gau. Frank continued to see her secretly.

In 1942 Himmler discovered that Frank had misappropriated funds and looted art, furs, and gold from Poland. Himmler demanded that Frank turn over control of the policing of Poland to the SS. This quickened the flow of Jews to concentration camps, most of whom went to Auschwitz. This action earned Frank the title, "Jew Killer of Cracow."

That same year President Roosevelt issued a list of war criminals; Frank was in the number one position. This fed Frank's ego, and he called a meeting of his staff to boast about it. He made certain that all his orders and activities were recorded by his secretary. Eventually, these records comprised forty-two bound volumes which Frank turned over to the Tribunal thinking that their contents would exonerate him. Instead, they helped convict him.

In prison Frank became a changed man. He believed that Hitler had mesmerized him and had produced a behavior within him that he could not account for. He stated that it was as if there were two Franks--the one in prison and the one during the war. The one in prison didn't understand how the one during the war could have behaved as he did. Frank frequently expressed remorse for his crimes and was baptized a Catholic while in prison. By all accounts his remorse and conversion were sincere.

He attempted suicide twice after his arrest--once by cutting his throat and once by cutting his wrist. The wound to the wrist was serious enough to cause nerve damage and withered his left hand. Frank wore a glove to hide this; he usually wore a scarf to cover the scar on his neck. He was bothered by the fluorescent lights in the courtroom, and he wore dark glasses. Unfortunately, this did not help his image; he was described by courtroom watchers as the most ominous man in the dock.

Frank was indicted on counts one, three, and four. He was found innocent on count one; guilty on counts three and four. He was sentenced to hang.

Arthur Seyss-Inquart was born in Czechoslovakia. His original surname was Zajtich, but he changed it when he immigrated to Austria and joined the Nazi party. He rose rapidly in its ranks and was appointed to serve under Hans Frank in Poland. He later became the Reich Commissioner of Holland, the equivalent of Frank's position. Seyss-Inquart had learned well from his former superior. He cleared Holland of virtually every Jew, including a young girl named Anne Frank who died at Bergen-Belsen.

Seyss-Inquart was not an imposing man. He was quiet and mild mannered in court and in prison. His distinguishing characteristics were a limp that he had acquired in a mountaineering accident and thick eyeglasses. He was intelligent, much more so than most of the other prisoners, and had the capability of examining the German behavior. He believed that Hitler's genius lay in an amalgamation of emotionalism and authority. The emotionalism appealed to the Southern Germans; the authority appealed to the Prussians.

Seyss-Inquart was indicted on all four counts; he was found guilty on counts two, three, and four and innocent on count one. He never denied his crimes and believed that he would be hung for them. He was right.

Hjalman Horace Greely Schact was the oldest and most intelligent of the prisoners. He had been Walter Funk's predecessor as Reichsbank President, where he used his financial genius to control Germany's inflation in the twenties and led it into a brief period of prosperity before the Great Depression.

Schact was a curious choice for a war criminal; he was not a member of Hitler's inner circle, and he had possessed no formal power for years. In fact, when he was arrested as a war criminal, he was a prisoner at Dachau where he had been sent for his supposed participation in the July Twentieth Plot to kill Hitler. Actually, he had hesitated in his decision long enough that the plot took place without his participation, but he was still arrested. The rational for his inclusion as a war criminal was that his financial schemes allowed Germany to re-arm itself.

Schact, who had been raised as an American and testified in English, maintained his innocence and stayed aloof from the other prisoners. He once stated that he was included as a criminal so that he could be acquitted and prove that the trial was fair.

Schact was indicted on counts one and two and found innocent on both. He was acquitted as he had predicted.

Walter Funk succeeded Hjmalmar Schact as President of the Reichsbank. He was a soft, round man with heavy jowls who had a weakness for the Epicurean life. Funk used his position as a top Nazi to indulge in fine cigars, liquor, and all night parties. He was married, but sought the company of young men for intimate engagements. He was afflicted with a weak bladder and frequently had to be escorted from the court to the men's room.

Funk tearfully confessed in prison to his major sin-depositing the confiscated assets of Jews into the Reichsbank. Those deposits included gold teeth yanked from the jaws of gassed corpses. Funk clearly knew how those teeth had been obtained and believed that the Jews had been killed primarily for their gold teeth which were used to finance the war.

Funk wept when he was indicted on all four counts. He wept in court as he viewed the evidence of the Reichsbank's vaults, which contained jewelry, eyeglasses, and teeth. He wept when he watched the concentration camp film.

He was indicted on all four counts and found guilty on counts two, three, and four. He was sentenced to life in prison, and he wept again.

Wilhelm Frick was Hitler's Minister of the Interior. He was sixty-nine years old, and he had spent most of those years promoting anti-Semitic legislation. He began introducing such in the Reichstag when Hitler was still in Landsberg Prison for conducting the Munich Putsch and continued until 1936 when he issued the Nuremberg Laws.

Frick actually made Hitler the Chancellor of Germany.

Since Hitler was not a German citizen and his application for citizenship had been denied because of his prison record, he could not hold office. Frick found a law stating that anyone appointed to an official post was entitled to citizenship. After several attempts and one bungle when Frick appointed Hitler to a position too low to suit him, Frick got Hitler named Councilor of Braunschweig. A year later Hitler was Chancellor. Frick believed that this was his proudest accomplishment. In 1933 he followed this accomplishment by helping pass the Enabling Laws which gave Hitler complete control of Germany.

Frick was familiar with concentration camp operations and knew of the death camps. He once said of the Jews that, "we turn them into fog." However, he was sickened by the concentration camp films shown in court and said that he didn't understand how things like that could have happened.

Frick continually wore a plaid jacket in prison and in court. He was described by court watchers as the most colorless man on trial. He was indicted on all four counts and found guilty on counts two, three, and four. He was sentenced to death.

Robert Ley was head of the German Labor Front, and, according to his colleagues, he performed his duties while constantly drunk. Unlike the other prisoners who brought several changes of clothes and other personal items to prison, Ley arrived with only the clothes on his back. He was issued army fatigues that were dyed black indicating that "they were unfit for any purpose."

Ley seemed disoriented in the exercise yard and was given to outbursts in his cell. When his indictment was read to him he screamed, "Why don't they stand us against the wall and shoot us? Why should we be brought before a tribunal like..." He broke off and was unable to say the word "criminals."

Ley never made it to the trial. He committed suicide in his cell by wrapping a towel around the pipe behind his toilet, looping it around his neck, and leaning forward. He stuffed his mouth with a rag to prevent himself from crying out. The toilet was the only part of the cell out of the guard's view, although the prisoner's legs were visible when he used the facility. The guard saw Ley's legs with their trousers bunched around his ankles and had no reason to be suspicious. When the legs did not move for several minutes, and Ley did not respond to his name, the guard summoned his superior. Ley was found dead.

Ley's suicide prompted immediate action from Colonel Andrus. Each prisoner was now watched every minute that he was in his cell instead of every two to three minutes. Spot lights were attached to the door grates, and the cells were fully illuminated at night. Random searches of the cells were conducted. Andrus was certain he had now made his prison suicide proof; there were, however, some variables that he could not control.

Admiral Karl Donitz was Grand Admiral of the German Navy and briefly head of the German post war government at Flensburg. Donitz was surprised when Hitler picked him as his successor. Goering as Reichmarshall was next in line after Hitler, but when Goering prematurely judged Hitler dead, he fell from Hitler's grace. Donitz's sense of duty required that he obey his Fuhrer's request.

Donitz was an able tactician and was known as the "Rommel of the Seas." He developed the wolf pack submarine strategy that sunk 2472 allied ships and allowed Germany to command the seas in the early part of the war. Donitz believed that he had commanded the Navy in a proper fashion and had fought an honorable war. He had, however, issued the Laconia Order which prohibited the navy from picking allied survivors from the ocean. The order included women and children. Donitz correctly argued in court that the order was not substantially different from the policy under which the United States operated. Although Donitz knew of the existence of the concentration camps and used workers from them in the ship yards, he probably did not know of their conditions.

Donitz was one of the more stylish prisoners and also one of the most emotionless. He had no outward reactions to his indictment, to the evidence presented in court, or to his sentence. Donitz was apparently practiced in controlling his feelings. His colleagues stated that he did not react when told of the deaths of both his sons. In fact, immediately following the notification of his second son's death, he attended a social function with his wife. She later collapsed.

Donitz was charged with counts one, two, and three and found guilty on counts two and three. He was sentenced to twenty years in prison.

Franz von Papen was Reich Chancellor before Hitler. He convinced President von Hindenberg to accept his resignation and name Hitler the new Chancellor. This was the only reason he was arrested as a war criminal; his support of Hitler started the Third Reich.

von Papen was an aristocrat and he looked like one even in prison. He kept himself aloof from the other prisoners and never doubted his innocence. He was defended by his son, who was considered one of Germany's ablest lawyers.

von Papen was indicted on counts one and two and found innocent on both counts. He was acquitted.

Baron Konstantine von Neurath had been Germany's Foreign Minister until 1938. That year he attended the Hossbach Conference and heard Hitler declare his intention to wage an aggressive war. von Neurath was appalled and stated his objections to Hitler. Hitler promptly replaced him with von Ribbentrop who was not likely to question Hitler's decisions. In 1939, von Neurath was given the titular position of Protector of Bohemia and Moravia in Czechoslovakia.

von Neurath was seventy-three years old during the trial, and the prison psychologists believed that he displayed signs of senility. He was arrested as a war criminal for two reasons. First, during his tenure as Foreign Minister, Germany violated many treaties. Second, in his position as Protector he made no attempt to control the Gestapo or SS and signed all the death orders brought to him without objection.

von Neurath was indicted on all four counts and found guilty on all four. He was sentenced to fifteen years in prison, but he was released in 1954 because of his of poor health. He died two years later at the age of eighty-three.

Erich Raeder had been Grand Admiral of the navy before Karl Donitz and may have been on trial for political reasons. At the end of the war the United States hunted down and arrested most of the war criminals. The ever competitive Soviets were determined not to be out done. They managed to find and arrest Raeder and Hans Fritzch. However, the Soviets went about the process in a backwards fashion. They arrested the men first then found the crimes that they may have committed.

Despite the method of his arrest, Raeder was not an innocent man. He had actively built up the navy, which violated the Treaty of Versailles. He had been instrumental in forming the plans to invade Norway. His biggest sin was his attendance at the Hossback Conference, where he heard Hitler announce his intention to wage an aggressive war. Raeder did not object to this announcement and stayed in service to his Fuhrer.

Raeder was not a favorite among the other prisoners.

When he was captured by the Soviets he made what became known as the Moscow Statement. In that statement he referred to Donitz as conceited and unqualified. He maintained that Donitz was ridiculed by all thinking men and was called "Hitlerboy Donitz." He described Goering as a man of "unimaginable vanity and immeasurable ambition." Goering's outstanding characteristics were "greed, wastefulness, and soft, unsoldierly manner." Raeder thought Field Marshall Keitel was a man of "immeasurable weakness," and would take any type of abuse from Hitler. Raeder was unconcerned when the Moscow Statement was read in court. He had no desire to continue his associations with those men, and he believed that he would be executed.

Raeder was indicted on counts one, two, and three and found guilty on all three counts. He wasn't executed as he had expected, but sentenced to life in prison.

Hans Fritzche was the radio Propaganda Chief in Goebbel's Propaganda Ministry. Like Raeder, he was captured by the Soviets and held as a war criminal while they looked for evidence of his crimes. There was scant evidence. Fritzche had used his voice to encourage the hatred of Jews, but no evidence could be found that he had any knowledge of their treatment in concentration camps. In fact, Fritzche was deeply disturbed by the concentration camp film that was shown in court. He doubted that Germany would ever be free from its shame for those crimes.

Fritzche was not an interesting defendant at the trial. He had no startling testimony and sat quietly in the dock. His chief contributions were to advise his fellow defendants to speak slowly and use short sentences to make the translation more accurate and to compose a letter to Colonel Andrus requesting that Major Henry Gerecke be allowed to remain as prison chaplain. He might be best remembered as the prisoner that

Julius Streicher spat on in response to Fritsche's criticism of Der Sturmer.

Fritzche was indicted on counts one, three, and four and found innocent on all counts. He was acquitted by the Tribunal, but he was later tried in a German court and sentenced to three years in prison.

Ernst Kaltenbunner had the distinction of being the only prisoner who actually operated the killing apparatus in the concentration camps. He became head of the Reich Central Security Office (RSHA), the Nazi's internal security force, after Reinhard Heydrich was assassinated. He was second only to Himmler in the SS and oversaw the operation of the concentration camps, including the death camps. His name appeared on thousands of death orders.

Kaltenbrunner took his position as RSHA head seriously and maintained the same level of ruthlessness established by Heydrich. He demanded a quota of one thousand Jews killed each day at Mathausen, a demand he enforced even when Berlin was being lost to the Allies. He wanted no inmates of any concentration camps alive to be liberated, and he devised partially fulfilled plans to accomplish this. One plan involved force marching all inmates to Dachau and dropping a bomb on them; another called for inmates to be sealed in a mine or cave and gassed.

Kaltenbrunner always created a stir in court, and he was a favorite of court watchers simply because his appearance matched preconceived notions of what a Nazi should look like. Most of the war criminals were slight men that resembled bank clerks. Kaltenbrunner loomed over the others with his six foot six inch frame and scarred face which seemed the very image of evil. Many people assumed that the scars were dueling scars; actually, they resulted when Kaltenbrunner ran his car into a tree while drunk.

Kaltenbrunner performed most of his duties while drunk. He was an Austrian and came from a family of lawyers. He worked his way through law school as a coal miner, and he identified closely with the working class. He joined the Nazi party in 1930, and, despite his legal training, operated like a thug. He beat up political opponents, destroyed property, and instigated riots. When Hitler appointed him to the RSHA the doctor who examined him declared him to be a "lummox" and "incapable of thought unless drunk." He was shunned by most of the prisoners; his own lawyer refused to shake his hand.

Despite his threatening visage, Kaltenbrunner was not strong either emotionally or physically. When he heard his indictment he sobbed uncontrollable and said, "I want my family." A few weeks before the trial he complained of headaches and suffered a stroke that was likely caused by fear and stress. He recovered sufficiently to participate in the trial, but his speech was marked by hesitations.

Kaltenbrunner was charged with counts one, three, and four. He was found guilty on counts three and four and sentenced to death.

Baldur von Schirach was the youngest prisoner. He was Hitler's youth leader and Gauleiter (District Party Chief) of Vienna. As the youth leader he had charge of nine million German boys and girls through a hierarchy of organizations. In 1939 when the older youths were being trained for war, he explained to them that they would be dying for Mozart. The ultimate purpose, military training, of the youth groups marked von Schirach as a war criminal.

His position as Gauleiter gave him a villa with seventeen servants. His first act in Vienna was to deport 60,000 Jews to

Poland to ease a housing shortage; most were sent to Auschwitz. He claimed that this act contributed to European culture. He repeatedly stated that he had no knowledge of what went on in the concentration camps, although as Gauleiter he received weekly extermination reports.

von Schirach was more American than German. His grandfather had lost a leg at the Battle of Bull Run in the Civil War and was an honorary pall bearer at Abraham Lincoln's funeral. His mother was a member of the Daughters of the American Revolution; the Tribunal received many letters from Americans, including influential DAR members, requesting clemency for von Schirach.

von Schirach's father was German and the director of the National Theater at Weimar. He provided his family with culture and privilege until Germany's economic collapse cost him his position. In his late teens von Schirach read Henry Ford's The International Jew, and this became the root of his anti-semitism. When he heard Hitler espouse the same beliefs, he became a Storm Trooper, one of its few members with education and culture.

von Schirach did not create a favorable impression on the prison staff. He was said to have looked like a homosexual or a child molester. The prison psychologist believed that von Schirach was capable of great self-delusion. Despite their emphasis on arms training, he stated that his youth groups were similar to the Boy Scouts. It was his self-delusion that led to his arrest. At the end of the war he had taken the name Richard Falk and was writing a novel in Vienna. The world believed that Baldur von Schirach was dead. When he learned that the war criminals were to be tried, he turned himself in and volunteered his talents to re-educate German youth for democracy.

von Schirach was indicted on counts one and four and found guilty on count four. He was sentenced to twenty years in prison.

Field Marshall Wilhelm Keitel was Chief of Staff of the armed forces and put Hitler's demands into orders. Unfortunately for Keitel, most of those demands were against the accepted rules of warfare and international law. Keitel signed orders approving the ruse that started the invasion of Poland and orders calling for the killing of Poland's intelligencia, clergy, and nobility. He ordered the assassination of two fugitive French generals. One of his most damning orders was the Commando Order which stated that all British Commando Troops were to be shot--no prisoners were to be taken. Equally damning were the Reprisal Order and the Commissar Order that were directed against Soviet guerrilla fighters. On the basis of these orders 2300 Soviet civilians were herded together and shot in retaliation for the deaths of ten German Einsatgruppen (death squad) members. Keitel also issued the Night and Fog Order against the French Resistance. The order earned its name because the suspects were arrested and executed in the middle of the night. They disappeared into the night and fog.

Keitel knew that those orders were wrong; on the stand he admitted that the Night and Fog Order was especially cruel. He knew that by ordering the assassination of the French generals he had violated the sacred tenet of a Prussian officer; that is, a general's person, friend or enemy, was inviolate. He stated that he didn't understand how he could have issued that order. The other criminals that were military men reproached him for it.

Keitel could not resist Hitler's influence. He resigned several times and tried to object to Hitler's demands but always caved. This might have been why Hitler appointed him Chief of Staff. Hitler wanted to control his generals, and Keitel could be controlled. He was, in fact, so well controlled that he was known as "Hitler's Lackey." It was said that Keitel automatically began nodding in agreement as soon as Hitler spoke. Hitler described him as "having the brains of a movie usher" and "as loyal as a dog."

Despite his forty-one years of military service, Keitel had never intended to be a career soldier. He had planned to be a gentleman farmer and had joined the military to wait out his inheritance, his father's estate at Helmscherade, Braunschweig. When his father died in 1934, he prepared to retire from the military and run the estate. Keitel's wife, impressed with the power and prestige of being a general's wife, demanded that he remain in the army.

In prison and in court Keitel's behavior was soldierly and stoic He wanted to plead his guilt, but Goering forbade it. Keitel obeyed the order. He also stood aside for Goering and clicked his heels whenever he approached. He refused to report any of his ailments to the prison doctor, but did confide to the psychologist that he had thought of suicide during the war. He was considered a suicide risk and was watched closely.

Keitel was indicted on all four counts and found guilty on all four. He was sentenced to death.

Colonel General Alfred Jodl was the Operations Chief of the German Armed Forces. He had the distinction of signing Germany's surrender at the Boys' Technical and Professional School at Rheims. At that time Jodl knew something was amiss; he was not treated with the deference traditionally accorded to a defeated general. Eisenhower had already seen the concentration camps.

Jodl worked with Keitel to put Hitler's demands into orders and policy. Those demands included the Commando Order and the Reprisal Order, both contrary to accepted warfare. Unlike Keitel, Jodl was one of the few people who disagreed with Hitler, and he formally protested Germany's actions at Malmedy. Nonetheless, he followed each of Hitler's requests. He accounted for this obedience by stating that he had been seduced by Hitler's early military successes and that he was trained to obey orders. He said that following orders was the code of his life.

Jodl may not have been completely happy fulfilling his code. He believed that Hitler considered him an errand boy, and he knew that Hitler had planned to replace him. Jodl's one admission was that he hated Hitler for his contempt of the middle class to which Jodl belonged, and his hatred of his general staff of which Jodl was a member. Yet, Jodl never abandoned his Fuhrer.

Jodl was described as cold and emotionless. The guards voted him the least popular prisoner not because he exhibited inappropriate or difficult behavior, but because he sat quietly in his cell and interacted with almost no one. Jodl did walk in the exercise yard with the other military men, Keitel, Donitz, and Raeder, but he remained reserved. He did not desire visits from the prison psychologist or chaplain. He did not wish to express an inner guilt or remorse or have his motives examined beyond the fact that he obeyed orders. He expected to be hung and accepted it. He never displayed emotion in court, but he did react to the concentration camp film by stating that "the camps were the most fearful heritage of the Nazis."

Jodl was indicted on all four counts and found guilty on all four. His sentence was death.

Ernst Friedrich Christoph (Fritz) Sauckel was named the Plenipotentiary General for the Allocation of Labor in 1942, and in that capacity he supplied the slave labor to operate Albert Speer's factories. As the war progressed, Speer needed a tremendous number of laborers to produce equipment and supplies. The Gauleiters, who had their own labor quotas, were reluctant to give up any workers. Speer complained to Hitler that he could not manage the factories and recruit laborers. He need an assistant and suggested Sauckel. Sauckel was surprised when Hitler announced his new position.

Sauckel succeeded as Plenipotentiary General as he had succeeded all his life--by hard work. When Speer's labor demands became more and more exorbitant, Sauckel worked harder to fulfill them. He was the only one of Hitler's inner circle that was from the working class. His father had been a mailman, and his mother had been a seamstress. Sauckel joined the merchant seamen at the age of fifteen; his ship was captured in World War I, and he spent those years in a French prison. He could not find employment in post war Germany, but his religious beliefs caused him to reject Communism. He found the Nazi Party and Hitler.

Sauckel made no pretense about having culture or education. He never read a book and was uncomfortable in social settings. He preferred to spend his free time with his wife and ten children. He was ostracized by most of Hitler's general staff; they considered him their errand boy, not a colleague. He was excluded from most high level meetings and called "saukerl" (jerk) by both Speer and Goebbels. Even when Sauckel styled his mustache after Hitler's, he was still not accepted.

The demands and ridicule by Hitler and Speer and others probably broke Sauckel. In 1944 he was found stowed away in the torpedo room of a U-boat. News of his presence was radioed to Admiral Donitz who ordered the U-boat's immediate return. Sauckel went back to work.

Sauckel was described as confused in court and in prison. At times, it seemed as if he didn't realize that Germany had lost the war. He didn't understand how he could be considered a war criminal, and he was more confused by why no one could accept the reasons for his innocence. He protested that he knew nothing about crimes against humanity and knew nothing about lawyers. On the stand he tried to convince the Tribunal that he had no control over the conditions suffered by his laborers. Speer had full control, he insisted. His protests bordered on whining, and he had no evidence to back his claims.

Sauckel was indicted on all four counts and found guilty on counts three and four. He was sentenced to death.

Alfred Rosenberg was a man who loved titles after his name. Three of his titles, Chief Philosopher, Reichminister of Eastern Territories, and Head of Einstab Rosenberg, caused him to be arrested as a war criminal.

As Chief Philosopher he tried to elevate anti-Semitism to a respectable philosophy. In his book, Myth of the Twentieth Century, he expounded on his theories of blood superiority. The book was considered unreadable even by Rosenberg's colleagues, but this was not a detraction. To the German mind unreadability equated with profound.

As Reichminister of the Eastern Territories he allowed his lethal racial philosophies to be put into practice. He stated in court that he still believed in ethnic cleansing, but he objected to the clumsy manner in which the concentration camp operators had achieved it.

The Einstab Rosenberg, which Rosenberg created and ran, was ostensibly organized to protect the art treasures of Europe for educational purposes after the war. In reality, it allowed the Nazis to loot anything they thought had value. Through the Einstab both Hitler and Goering amassed huge collections; Goering bragged that he had the largest private collection of art in Europe. When the Nazis invaded Paris nearly

70,000 Jewish homes were stripped of everything of value. Thirty thousand railroad cars were need to transport the booty to Germany.

Rosenberg persisted in his blood superiority theories in prison; he presented the psychologist with an essay on the American Negro. In it he urged that all Negroes be returned to Africa. Otherwise, he predicted, in one hundred fifty years the white race would be obliterated from the United States. The psychologist believed that Rosenberg's personality disintegrated in prison and that he was a suicide risk. Rosenberg's most persistent complaint was that sleeping with his hands outside his blanket, which was a security requirement, made his hands cold.

Rosenberg was indicted on all four counts and found guilty on all four. He was sentenced to death.

Julius Streicher was Gauleiter of Franconia, which included Nuremberg, but he was best known for publishing Der Sturmer, an anti-Semitic newspaper. Streicher had a long history of anti-Semitism and had spent time in Nuremberg Prison for beating and killing Jews before the Nazis came into power.

Streicher abused his position as Gauleiter even by Nazi standards; he kept all the profits from confiscated Jewish property for himself. Der Sturmer, which Streicher considered to be the official publication of Nazism, was hated by most ranking Nazis because it robbed the party of what little respectability it had. The paper, which was written at the comic book level, made such outrageous claims as the Virgin Mary was a whore, that all Jews molested Christian children, and that Streicher had devised a divining rod to distinguish the Jews from the Gentiles. However, its most common theme, that of an older Jewish man seducing an innocent Christian girl, may have had some affinity for Hitler. It is believed that Hitler's grandmother, who worked as a domestic in a Jewish household, was seduced in that manner.

When Streicher claimed in Der Sturmer that Goering's daughter was conceived by artificial insemination, Goering demanded an investigation of Streicher. He was found to be unfit for any type of human leadership, and in 1940 he was stripped of all party posts and power. He adopted the name of Seiler, secluded himself on a farm near Berchtegaden and spent the remaining war years painting pictures.

In prison Streicher was a pariah, shunned by both prison personnel and fellow prisoners. Frick complained that he had to sit next to him in court. His personal habits repelled the guards; he exercised completely nude and washed himself in the toilet bowl. Streicher tested at the lowest intelligence level, dull normal, of all the prisoners, but displayed more than a passable ability at sketching, the activity with which he filled his time. Streicher arrived with only the clothes on his back; he traded his autograph for sticks of gum. At the end of the trial but prior to being sentenced, Streicher stated that he wanted to join the Jews in their fight for their new homeland, Israel. Their scrappiness now impressed him.

Streicher was indicted on counts one and four and found guilty on count four. He was sentenced to death.

Joachim von Ribbentrop was Hitler's Foreign Minister, although by his own admission, he knew nothing of Germany's foreign policy. His lack of knowledge and analytical ability was precisely the reason that Hitler named him to the post. When von Neurath resigned as Foreign Minister after Hitler openly declared his intention to wage war, Hitler wanted a minister that he could manipulate. von Ribbentrop fit that requirement.

von Ribbentrop studied to be a musician, and he was talented at playing the violin. At seventeen he emigrated to Canada to continue his musical career, but returned to Germany when World War I started. After the war he married the daughter of a champagne magnate and became familiar with the upper class. Apparently, the upper class and nobility impressed him; at the age of thirty-two he arranged for an aunt whose husband had been knighted to adopt him. This allowed him to be titled and use the "von." This act of vanity and social climbing earned him the scorn of most legitimately titled persons, but he insisted on using the "von."

von Ribbentrop joined the Nazis in 1932 when Hitler became the main political force ln Germany. Through his social connections von Ribbentrop moved into Hitler's circle and was appointed as ambassador to Britain. He was not effective and regarded as a pompous fool by most Britains, but he correctly mouthed Nazi propaganda. This loyalty earned him his appointment as Foreign Minister.

As Foreign Minister his only significant contribution was the formulation of the Soviet Pact. This was the single occasion when Hitler had listened to his advice. The remainder of von Ribbentrop's tenure was marked by his acquiescence to Hitler's demands and the autocratic treatment of his staff. He demanded that his entire staff greet him at the airport or train station when he returned from a trip. If his plane or train were delayed, even for several hours, he expected them to remain and wait for his arrival. When Hitler violated the Soviet Pact, von Ribbentrop confronted Hitler and objected. Hitler responded with such a fury that von Ribbentrop actually became ill and took to his bed with temporary paralysis of his left side. He suffered with a continual headache for the next five years. He never stood up to Hitler again.

von Ribbentrop deteriorated badly in prison. His cell was piled with documents that he continually leafed through hoping to find the one document that would clear him. Guards complained of the odor emanating from both von Ribbentrop and his cell. He badgered the guards and had conflicts with his lawyers; his first lawyer quit in disgust. He complained that the cell block was too noisy for him to sleep, but he refused to take a sedative offered by the prison doctor. During the trial he sent a letter to the Tribunal offering to be tortured to atone for Germany's sins. Despite the abuse von Ribbentrop suffered from Hitler and despite his current situation, he refused to denounce Hitler. von Ribbentrop claimed that if Hitler appeared to him in his cell he would follow him anywhere.

von Ribbentrop was indicted on all four counts and found guilty on all four. He was sentenced to death.

Rudolf Hess was Deputy Fuhrer, the third highest Nazi in Germany, but in 1941 he flew to Scotland and spent the rest of the war in prison. Although he had almost no role in the war, the Soviets insisted that he be indicted on all counts. The purpose of Hess' trip was to unite Germany and Britain in a war against the Soviet Union. The British thought Hess was mad and at times confined him to a mental hospital; the Soviets thought he was the most diabolical of the war criminals.

Hess was born in Egypt and did not emigrate to Germany until he was fourteen. He loved Egypt and years later he would wax poetic about its beauties. During World War I he served in the same regiment as Hitler, although the two never met. Hitler remained with the same regiment throughout the war; Hess soon moved on and by the end of the war he was a pilot. He loved flying; Egypt and flying were probably the only things that Hess was passionate about. After the war he attended the first rally of the Nazi Party, and on July 1, 1920, he became the sixteenth person to join. He marched with Hitler in the Munich Putsch, was arrested, and sent to Landsberg Prison along with Hitler. In prison Hitler and Hess had many discussions and some believe that Hess wrote most of Mein Kampf, although this is probably not true. Hess did give Hitler the idea of lebensraum (living space) for Germans, and Hitler later used the concept as justification for invading most of Europe. When they were released from Landsberg, Hitler named him Deputy Fuhrer, second in command, and Hess managed the bureaucracy of the party. He read and approved every law and wrote every decree. He stayed by Hitler's side until his flight to Scotland.

To call Hess odd would be generous. Although Hess successfully feigned amnesia during his imprisonment in England and during his initial incarceration at Nuremberg, his behavior had been markedly different from his colleagues for years. Some suggested that his strange behavior resulted from being hit in the head with a brick during the Munich Putsch. Hess never smoked or drank and refused to socialize. It is likely that Hitler arranged his marriage--a marriage in which a child was not conceived for ten years. In the thirties Hess became a vegetarian and promoted non-medical cures; he established a hospital for quacks. His oddities cost him his position. When Hitler visited the Hess household in the late thirties, he decided that Hess was unfit to rule Germany. Goering was named second in command, and Hess found himself being moved outside Hitler's circle. His flight to Scotland was his last desperate bid for influence.

Hess displayed such aberrant behavior at Nuremberg that he convinced the psychologist that he was insane. He goosed stepped around the exercise yard and insisted in eating while prostrate on the floor. He claimed not to recognize either his wife or Goering; he wrote, "I can't remember," at the bottom of his indictment. Hess' mental stability was one of the first concerns of the Tribunal. The psychologist, who believed that Hess' amnesia and insanity were real, explained to Hess that he would probably not be tried and moved to another prison. In court Hess signaled his lawyer and passed him a note stating that his memory had returned, and his mind was functioning well. Apparently, the thought of being isolated from his colleagues as he had been in England was more than he could bear.

Hess' behavior continued to be different. His cell was

nearly as messy as von Ribbentrop's, and he read novels in court. He refused to be cross examined, which may have been a tactical move to keep from revealing his early activities in the Nazi Party.

Hess was indicted on all four counts and found guilty on counts one and two. He was sentenced to life in prison. When he died in 1987, possibly by his own hand, he was ninety-three years old and the last war criminal.

Albert Speer was Hitler's Armaments Minister and managed the factories and bureaucracy needed to supply the German military with weapons as well as to develop new technology to fight the Allies. Speer was tremendously successful in his role; so successful that the Allied nations valued his knowledge. At the end of the war Speer delivered several lectures on his methods and on Germany's technical progress, especially its progress towards the production of atomic weapons. In his lectures he prudently omitted that fact that his factories were staffed by slave laborers. He had completed such a lecture in Frankfurt just minutes before his arrest as a war criminal. Speer was surprised. He had hoped that his knowledge would secure his freedom, and he imagined that he would become a consultant to England and America.

Speer's life revolved around technology; he once stated that machines were more real to him than people. He was born into a family of architects, and he continued the tradition. He was teaching architecture at the Institute of Technology in Berlin in 1931 when he attended a lecture given by Hitler next door to his classroom. Speer was fascinated by Hitler, and he joined the party. Hitler was impressed by Speer's talent and through the thirties Speer designed and built several Nazi District Headquarters, the stage for the Nuremberg Rallies, the grandstand at Zeppelin Field, the Reich Chancellory, and Hitler's private residence in Berlin. To accomplish this, Speer spent hours alone with Hitler, perhaps more than any other person.

This created a rivalry between Speer and Goering, a rivalry that persisted until they were sentenced at Nuremberg. Hitler named him Armaments Minister in 1942 to replace Fritz Todt who had died in a plane crash. Speer then controlled twelve million workers, most of whom were slave laborers.

Speer may have loved technology and machines, but he was also charming. He had refinement and treated everyone with courtesy. It would have been difficult to find anyone who did not like Speer. Hitler liked him; the generals of the July Twentieth Plot liked him although Speer did not join them; the Gauleiters liked him, and the Allies like him. He even made a favorable impression on the wife of the British prosecutor.

Speer used his charm and ability to solve problems to avoid the death penalty. He perceived almost immediately that the Tribunal was impressed by admissions of guilt and words of repentance, as opposed to the defiance that was advocated by Goering. Speer was suitably contrite when he heard his indictment and worked with the prison psychologist to bring the other prisoners to his penitent philosophy. Speer suggested to the psychologist that Goering be isolated from the other prisoners to reduce his influence. He was fluent in English and frequently assisted the translators in court. All of this made a favorable impression on the Tribunal.

While Speer was making a good impression, he calculated his admissions and carefully observed the prosecutors. Although he knew of the horribly inhuman conditions in his factories and concentration camps, he shifted much of that blame to Fritz Sauckel. He stated that he had, on his own, attempted to kill Hitler, although no proof of this existed. He neglected to mention that he wept openly when Hitler died. Speer noticed that Robert Jackson, although the lead prosecutor, was no longer adept at cross examinations. Speer had been scheduled to be cross examined by one of Jackson's staff, a more able questioner.

Speer suggested that since Goering had been cross examined by Jackson, he should be too, in order to keep his status as leader of the penitent prisoners. His suggestion was accepted, and Jackson did a lackluster job.

Speer's calculations worked; he was saved from the death penalty. However, if he knew that the reason the Tribunal gave him a prison sentence was that they felt that he had an immature personality and was given to hero worship, he might not have been pleased.

Speer was indicted on all four counts and found guilty on counts three and four. He was sentenced to twenty years in prison.

Hermann Goering was Reichmarshall, second in command, and the Allies' prize prisoner; if Hitler could not be made to pay for the war, Goering would. Goering was not captured; he turned himself in. In the last days of the war he was certain that Hitler had died in Berlin, and he announced that he was in command. Hitler, who wasn't dead yet, heard the announcement and ordered Goering to be shot on sight. Goering made his way to the American lines and surrendered. He arrived with sixteen pieces of matching luggage, a valet, assorted jewelry, and large supply of men's cosmetics, about 20,000 paracodine pills, of which he took twenty a day, and several cyanide capsules. He was grossly obese; his short frame carried nearly 270 pounds.

Goering and Andrus quickly developed a mutual hatred. Andrus could not stand Goering's addiction and gluttony, and he placed him on a diet and weaned him from the paracodine. This may have been a mistake; without his excess weight and addiction to make him lethargic, Goering's energy and wit returned, and he became a formidable opponent in court and in prison. Andrus believed that Goering was a homosexual, an idea largely based on Goering's ample use of cosmetics and penchant for colorful uniforms. Andrus spread the rumors that Goering wore rouge and lipstick and painted his toenails. Goering believed himself to be an historic figure and considered Andrus a lowly jailer. Goering used his status as the most important war criminal to manipulate Andrus' regulations and taunt the prison personnel.

Goering's mother had said that he would either be a great man or a criminal; he matched both her expectations. He graduated from the Military Academy at Gross Lichterfelch, the German equivalent of West Point, summa cum laude and was a flying ace in World War I. His number of kills was second only to the Red Baron. He was awarded the Blue Max, and at the age of twenty-one, he commanded the Flying Circus. After the war he joined the Nazi party and worked as an air taxi pilot. On one trip he flew to the estate of Carin von Kartzow; they fell in love and began a torrid affair. Hitler, ever the prude, demanded that Goering either marry the woman or end the affair. In 1923 Carin von Kartzow left her husband and estate and married Goering. Later that year Goering was wounded in the groin when he marched with Hitler in the Munich Putsch. He was nursed back to health by two Jewish sisters, but he became addicted to morphine. Goering and his wife spent the next several years traveling Europe and living on her money. His addiction worsened, and he attempted suicide. His treatment at a drug clinic failed, and he was placed in an asylum where he spent his days ranting against Jews. When he was released he begged Hitler to get him elected to the Reichstag. He was elected in 1928 and immediately began taking bribes from transportation contractors.

Goering firmly established his influence with Hitler by engineering the Roehm Purge. Roehm, who was the head of the Storm Troopers, thought that Hitler was betraying Nazism. One of Roehm's main objections was that Hitler tolerated a man as corrupt as Goering. Goering manufactured a list of disloyal Storm Troopers and pictures of Roehm in homosexual trysts. Hitler had his excuse to kill Roehm. Hitler rewarded Goering by naming him head of the Luftwaffe (Air Force).

Goering may have been as driven to impress his wife as Hans Frank was to impress Lilli Gau. When Goering's wife died of a weak heart in 1931, he tearfully admitted that all his manipulations, boasting, and machinations were done to provide Carin with a life as good as the one she had left for him. Goering did marry again, but his second wife always lived in the shadow of Carin's memory.

Goering may have been a flying ace, but he was a failure as a manager. The Luftwaffe was disorganized and inefficient. He kept Hitler placated with boasts and promises. He bragged that no Allied plane could penetrate German air space; an empty boast as the bomb damage in ever major German city attested. Because of the failure of the Luftwaffe he lost most of his influence with Hitler. When Germany's defeat was obvious, Hitler stated that the failed Luftwaffe was the chief cause. Goering's re-addiction to paracodine in 1937 may have been a reason for his ineptitude.

Although Goering was a failure at running the Luftwaffe, he was skilled at satisfying his own desires. Through the Einstab Rosenberg, he stole most of the art in Europe which he secreted in a salt mine at Obersalzberg. He also looted huge quantities of liquor, cigars, and foodstuffs. Goering admitted in court that his collecting may have gotten out of hand. He also admitted to re-arming Germany against the Treaty of Versailles, to knowing about the conditions of the concentration camps, and to the elimination of the Jews. He denied nothing, but justified his actions through the Nazi philosophy. He appeared unaffected by the concentration camp films and films of the slaughters by the death squads in the Soviet Union. He questioned the authenticity of the films and said that he had seen so much death in World War I that such pictures couldn't terrify him. He was formidable in court and completely flustered Jackson during his cross examination. Goering was especially adept at comparing Germany's crimes to the failures of the Allied nations. When questioned about the Nazi's anti-Semitism, he pointedly noted America's treatment of blacks.

Goering's defiance and unrepentant attitude made him popular. Contrite admissions of guilt may have impressed the Tribunal, but Goering's refusal to repent pleased the press, spectators, and the guards. It was feared that his popularity might spill over to the German people and that he would become a martyr to the Nazi cause.

Goering was voted the most popular prisoner by the guards. This was no accident; Goering went out of his way to curry their favor. They were perhaps the only people that Goering treated with courtesy. He inquired about their duties, families, and their favorite pastime, baseball. He bestowed gifts of his personal belongings on several. Goering had an ulterior motive for this behavior. He had cyanide capsules hidden in his luggage which was kept in a storage room at the end of the cell block. Friendly guards were more likely to give Goering access to the storage room or fetch particular items for him.

Although Goering was popular among the guards, he was not popular with the other prisoners. He felt that all the prisoners should present a united front and admit no wrong doing. He badgered the prisoners during meals and in the exercise yard. Some prisoners, mostly the military men, remained in his control throughout the trial; Keitel always stepped aside to let Goering pass. Others seemed ready to make confessions until they spent an hour with Goering. When he was isolated from the other prisoners, he begged to be allowed to eat with them. He claimed he was only trying the boost their spirits, not direct their thinking.

Goering was indicted on all four counts and found guilty on all four. He was sentenced to death.

Goering never made the walk to the gallows. On October 15, 1946, just hours before the official execution, Goering slipped a cyanide capsule into his mouth and sucked in the poison. Attempts to revive him were futile. How Goering come into possession of the capsule remains a mystery. He did arrive at Bad Mondf, the initial facility for war criminals, with a supply, and he sacrificed some to misdirect the guards for others. Goering had the capsule in his luggage in the storage room, but how he got it into his cell will probably never be known. The prisoners' cells were subject to random searches, and one was conducted the day before his death. It is speculated that Goering hid the capsule under the rim of the toilet pipe, in his naval, in his anus, and in his mattress. At the beginning of his confinement he was overweight, and his naval cavity was deep and could be closed off by his blubber. He probably concealed at least one capsule there when he entered prison. As his weight dropped he lost the fat that held the capsule in place, and he shifted it to his anus. Minute quantities of fecal mater on the capsule confirm his anus as a hiding place. The fact that he took the capsule while lying in bed suggests that it was finally secreted into the mattress.

Goering left four notes, all misdated. In the one directed to Colonel Andrus he stated that he had had the capsule during his entire confinement, but Andrus was not clever enough to find it. This probably was a last stab at a hated enemy, and the point is moot; he is as dead as his fellow criminals.

Where Goering hid the capsules might have been moot, but his means of death was not. Besides making Andrus look like a pompous buffoon, his suicide was considered a noble deed by some Germans. When his suicide was revealed several hours after the executions, crowds of Germans shouted, "Unser Hermann" (Our Hermann). One German official stated that, "You cannot take what is ours," which indicated the general dissatisfaction of Germans towards the Nuremberg Trial. Reporters stated that there was a consensus that Goering "put one over on the Allies."

This consensus apparently was not unanimous. A few hours before the official executions, Goering was hung in effigy near the Nuremberg Castle by a group of German children. Perhaps this represented hope; the younger generation was rejecting the Nazi heroes.

When I first learned of the atrocities that occurred in the concentration camps I wondered, along with most of the rest of the world, how so many people could have participated in such grossly aberrant behavior. I followed the trial and read the reported testimony of the defendants and the descriptions of their crimes. The trial was frequently a topic of discussion at the officers clubs. No one seemed to be able to account for the heinous behavior of the German people. Most Americans, including myself, had had numerous contacts with German citizens, and most of us found them to be cooperative and industrious. American soldiers liked the Germans, and it was difficult to reconcile the crimes described at Nuremberg with the polite people who seemed to want to please us.

I'm not sure that anyone can adequately explain what happened to the German society under Hitler and during the war, but I developed some thoughts as the trial progressed.

First, I had to believe that Hitler had enormous power to influence people. Several of the war criminals stated that Hitler "mesmerized" or "seduced" them into complying with his wishes, even when they knew those wishes were against the law and reasonable decency. Hitler could speak to massive crowds and hold their rapt attention for hours. He said once that a great orator made a great leader. Hitler could sway people, individually or in mass, and he used that ability to attain and keep his power.

Second, by the beginning of the war Hitler had surrounded himself with "yes" men who made no opposition to his demands. Anyone who had dared disagree with Hitler found himself without his position or without his life. Hitler's inner circle was composed of weak toadies such as Keitel and von Ribbentrop, of hopelessly corrupt men such as Goering, Frank, and Funk who reveled in their material wealth and of men who were thugs such as Kaltenbrunner who probably would have been a low level gangster in another society. There was no one to control Hitler's madness.

Neither of these two ideas accounted for the behavior of ordinary Germans who were physically removed from Hitler and his power group. Why would they obey such orders as to gas a thousand people a day? Surely, I thought, anyone would know that such an order could not be proper. Surely, anyone stationed at a concentration camp would know that its conditions were horribly wrong. Surely, every German knew what happened to the Jews and other in those camps. After all, millions of people simply do not disappear. Why didn't the Germans protest? Why did they kill their countrymen? Why did they allow and help the Nazi madness to proliferate?

I decided that there were several reasons that might explain the behavior of the German people. One of the most important was the rabidly anti-Semitic philosophy of the Nazi Party. For a generation the Germans heard the Jews denigrated, ridiculed, and vilified. They were made enemies of the state, of the German culture, and of Christianity. With such indoctrination the Germans accepted the imprisonment and elimination of the Jews as a patriotic necessity.

Germans were also indoctrinated to follow orders; they were trained to believe that their superiors were correct and never to question their decisions. The trait that American soldiers saw as cooperativeness was actually blind obedience, which is perfect behavior in a tyrannical society.

I think the final and perhaps most important reason was fear. Hitler was an all powerful dictator; anyone who opposed him vanished. This fear permeated the ranks of all Germans. Hitler terrorized his staff; his staff terrorized the Gaulieters and concentration camp operators, and those men terrorized the enlisted soldiers and citizens. The lowly soldier probably knew it was wrong to kill a thousand people a day and to have bodies stacked several feet high, but fear, especially the fear that he could be one of the thousand people, prevented him from objecting. I decided that Hitler's Germany could not have been a pleasant place for anyone.

CHAPTER TEN

From Landsberg to Nuremberg

On October 1, 1946, the Tribunal announced their verdicts. As expected, several death sentences were handed down; eleven men would hang. On October 3rd, I sat in Colonel Clayton's office, and he informed me that the date for the executions would be in the early morning hours of October 16th. The date, he said, was tentative, but if he did not notify me of any changes within forty-eight hours of the sixteenth, the date would be fixed. Colonel Clayton stressed that the date was top secret; no one knew it except me, Woods, the M.P.'S, and the appropriate prison personnel. The colonel emphasized the importance of secrecy as he had in my briefing in August. He wanted to avoid any possibility of protests, demonstrations, or chance that the criminals could achieve martyr status.

Colonel Clayton described the plan that we would follow. Woods, myself, and the M.P.'s would arrive at the Palace of Justice under the cover of darkness, set up the gallows, perform the executions, dismantle the gallows, and leave Nuremberg as soon as possible on the sixteenth. Orders would be given to Woods and the M.P.'s that would assign them to the guard detachment at Nuremberg prison. The colonel explained that he wanted their presence at the prison to look like a normal transfer of personnel, not like the arrival of an execution team. I would be given orders placing me on leave with arrangements allowing me to stay at the Grand Hotel which was near the Palace of Justice. I was to leave for Landsberg as soon as possible and

111

make whatever arrangements were necessary for the trip to Nuremberg. My orders to make those arrangements would again be verbal. No one would have any written orders assigning them to the actual execution. The colonel hoped that this arrangement would prevent leaks to the press and any German groups that might try to stop the executions. I would receive my next instructions through a telephone call from the colonel.

I settled my affairs in Heidelberg, and on Monday, October 7th, I picked up the faux orders for myself and the M.P.'s, and drove my jeep to Landsberg. I arrived in the early evening and met with Woods in the prison workshop. The gallows, he said, were completed, and they were ready for final assembly and testing. He suggested that we use the prison courtyard for those activities. He said he was ready to start in the morning. I agreed and returned the my quarters at the 47th Infantry.

The next morning, October 8th, I drove the short distance to the prison in a cold rain. The rain gave way to an equally cold mist as I met with Woods and the men in the workshop. I told them about our tasks and impressed upon them that the utmost secrecy was required. I told them not to discuss our activities even among themselves lest someone overhear. I also explained that from this point on all work would be done by us; no help from German prisoners would be permitted. Woods took charge of the meeting and directed the men to the courtyard to begin assembling the gallows.

The gallows were in three parts, the framework, which needed to be bolted together, the platform, and the steps which were in one piece. When completed, the platform stood eight feet high, and the thirteen steps were secured to its front. The area below the platform where the body would drop was obscured by a black curtain. The trap door was in the center of the platform, and the hangman's handle to release the door was to the rear of the platform. The framework formed a square arch several feet over the platform and had a large eye bolt in its center to secure the rope. The overall height of the gallows was fifteen feet, and the platform was eight feet wide.

Woods and I timed the assembly of the first gallows, and we estimated that about eleven or twelve hours would be needed to assemble all three. Woods spent the remainder of that day and all of the next testing the gallows, stretching his ropes, and tying the nooses. By October 10, thirteen ropes, one for each prisoner and two extra, eleven black hoods, which Woods made himself, and the leather boot laces and army web belts to secure the prisoners' hands and feet were packed into four duffel bags and stowed along with the personal duffel bags of the men. We were ready.

On the same day Colonel Clayton called and told me that the sixteenth of October was the firm date for the executions and that we were to arrive at Nuremberg in the early morning hours of the fourteenth. He had requested three semi-trailer trucks from the Munich quartermaster depot to transport the gallows; the trucks were to arrive on the morning of the thirteenth. He told me to have a stencil cut that corresponded to the Nuremberg quartermaster depot. He wanted the Munich code removed from the trucks and replaced with he Nuremberg code. That way, he said, the trucks would appear to be a local convoy carrying supplies, a common sight throughout Germany. He also told me not to try to find the Palace of Justice myself. He gave me the location of an intersection outside Nuremberg where I would meet a representative of the prison who would escort us through the city. The colonel didn't want to chance the possibility that we would get lost and call undo attention to ourselves. He explained that he had allowed about twenty-four hours extra travel time in case we encountered unforeseen difficulties. I thanked him and told him that the gallows were ready, the men were prepared, and that I anticipated no problems.

113

I didn't expect any problems. Woods and the men had prepared the gallows and all necessary equipment. I had marked my route on the map and had noted several landmarks to guide me. All we had to do was transport the gallows to Nuremberg and set them up, and we had more than ample time for those tasks. Woods and I spent some time in the next couple of days reviewing the jobs that each man would perform, but mostly we all relaxed. I drank a few beers and killed time with Lieutenant Holguin; Woods and a couple of the other men had dates.

On the morning of October 13th, we gathered in the prison courtyard. The gallows were dismantled and ready to be loaded; we just needed the trucks. I calculated that if the trucks left Munich at 0800 hours, they should arrive in Landsberg by 1000 hours. That would give us the afternoon to load, and we could start for Nuremberg by dusk and arrive shortly after midnight, which would make us right on schedule.

The morning was cold with a persistent drizzle, and after a few minutes we abandoned the courtyard and huddled by the stove in the workshop. By 1100 hours the trucks had not arrived, and I was anxious. I left the workshop to peer down the road, but no trucks were in sight. Woods noticed my agitation and said, "They'll get here, Lieutenant."

"Should have been here by now. They only had to come forty miles," I said.

"Roads aren't that great and the weather is bad. They could have
been held up by anything."

"I guess. We still have plenty of time. I won't worry for awhile, yet."

After lunch I was worried, and I walked to the small

office the Lieutenant Holguin had in the army wing of the prison and used his phone to call the quartermaster in Munich. This was not simply a matter of dialing a phone and requesting an extension. At that time Germany's phone system was little better than a string and tin cans. I had to request an operator and that operator had to wait for a line to open and then hope the call was directed to the right place. After a long wait and two misdirected calls, I talked to a sergeant at the depot who said the trucks had left Munich at 0800 hours and hadn't returned. He figured that they must be lost. I thought that was a lame excuse, but I bit my tongue and reminded the sergeant that the trucks had been requested by Colonel Clayton for a priority mission, and that they had to be in Landsberg as soon as possible. The sergeant assured me he'd send three more trucks out immediately.

I returned to the workshop; the men had started a poker game by the stove. When I entered Woods folded his hand, and we stepped into the courtyard.

"Munich sent them out this morning," I said. "They think they got lost."

"Lost," Woods snorted. "Those guys probably stopped off for some
German tail."

"Maybe. Anyway Munich sent three more trucks. They should be
here by 0300 hours."

"Let's hope so, Lieutenant." Woods turned back to the game and muttered over his shoulder, "Leave it to the army to screw things up."

By 0400 the second set of trucks had not arrived, and things were screwed up. I had been placed in charge of one of the most important post-war operations, and it was turning to crap. I could hear Colonel Clayton reaming me out. I could feel him pulling my bars off my collar and see him tearing up my commission papers. My picture would be in every paper with the caption, "Second Lieutenant Stanley Tilles causes delay in long awaited hangings." In desperation I walked to Holguin's office to call Munich.

After a delay of ten minutes I spoke to the same sergeant. I demanded to speak to his duty officer, but was told that he was unavailable.

"Sergeant, your second set of trucks haven't arrived."

"They must have gotten lost, too, Lieutenant."

"You have six trucks wandering the German country side and they are all lost?"

"I guess so, sir."

"Sergeant, I need those trucks. Find someone who knows where
Landsberg is and get them here."

"I don't think we can do that today, sir. All the men are off
duty. We could try again in the morning."

If the sergeant said anything else, I couldn't hear it because my heart was pounding in my ears. I forced myself calm, and with as steady a voice as I could manage I said, "Sergeant, those trucks are needed for a mission of international importance. If that mission gets screwed up even slightly, my butt will be chewed off. When that happens I'm certain to mention your incompetence. Do you understand what I am

116

saying to you, Sergeant?"

I heard a meek, "Yes, sir."

"I don't care if you have to drive all three trucks yourself. You get them here, and get them here now."

I didn't wait for an answer, but tossed the receiver at the phone.

I walked to the enlisted men's mess that was adjacent to the prison and picked at some dinner and wondered how, after all our preparations, the entire operation could be ruined by drivers that couldn't find the city of Landsberg. Landsberg was only forty miles from Munich, I muttered to the creamed corn on my plate. How in God's name could anyone get lost in just forty miles, I wondered. That thought reminded me that I still had to drive 110 miles to Nuremberg, and that didn't raise my spirits at all.

It was dark when I left the mess and walked to the prison. It was still drizzling, and it was cold; I zipped my jacket to my throat and hunched my shoulders against the wind. Woods and the men were still playing poker by the stove. He approached when I entered.

"They sent a third set out. They should arrive in an hour or so if they don't get lost, too," I said.

"Jesus, how could they screw up so bad?" Woods asked.

"I don't know. I had to threaten them to get this third set. They were going to wait until tomorrow."

"Tomorrow? My God, don't they know what we're doing?"

"No, John, they don't. Nobody knows but us."

"Yeah, that's right. Sorry. Lieutenant." He looked at his watch.
"Well, if they make good time, we should be all right. You know we'll all work like hell to make it on time."

That made me feel a little better, and I sat by the stove and watched the men shuffle and deal the cards for several hands. The repetitive flash of cards and the warmth of the stove mesmerized me, and I might have dozed. When I heard the blast from an air horn, I wasn't sure if it was real or if I was dreaming.

I knew the second blast was real, and I dashed out of the workshop and across the courtyard to the prison gate. The semis sat belching black exhaust into the drizzle. They came, I thought, and we can still make it. I felt like shouting for joy, but instead guided the drivers into the courtyard. Woods had already organized the men to load the gallows. I returned to the workshop to get my map and have a final cup of coffee.

The coffee was just beginning to warm my stomach when one of the men opened the door and said, "You better come, sir. The drivers won't let us load up."

I threw the remains of my coffee into the stove and trotted out to the courtyard. How could I be so unlucky in one day? I finally get the trucks, and now I have drivers that won't drive. Right then I was frustrated and angry enough to force them to load and drive under gun point.

As soon as I reached the courtyard I heard a steady flow of loud profanity. I joined Woods who had a big grin on his face.

118

I followed his line of sight and saw the source of the profanity. The lead driver, a sergeant, was dressing down the other drivers in the most vitriolic manner that I had ever witnessed. The men cringed from his insults and cowered against their trucks.

"What's going on?" I asked.

"Couple of the drivers figured out right off what we were loading. Started talking about how it's bad luck to carry gallows and how everyone was going to be killed. The sergeant caught wind of what was happening and he's really giving it to them. I'll bet now they'll drive to the moon if he told them to."

"Well, bless his heart " I said. "I was just about to shoot all of them."

"I'd have been right there with you, sir."

All of us worked like hell, but it was 0100 hours, the time that we should have arrived at Nuremberg, before the trucks were loaded and the Nuremberg depot code painted on their bumpers. Since our two jeeps were loaded with men, their gear, and the ropes and hoods, I decided to take my personal jeep. At the time I thought it was a logical decision; we needed another vehicle, and mine was readily available. Later, I realized that my two tone blue jeep with bright red seat covers probably looked odd leading a convoy of trucks. Fortunately, it didn't raise anyone's suspicions.

We had traveled no more than a few miles from Landsberg when we again encountered bad luck. The drizzle finally turned into a drenching rain. Army jeeps, as well as army trucks, had rudimentary wiper systems and no defrosting mechanisms. It became a challenge to wipe the windshield and stay on the road. Locating the landmarks that I had planned to guide me was next to impossible. I kept the convoy pointed north, and I hoped that Nuremberg was at the end of the road.

Sometime before dawn I believed that I had reached the intersection where we were to meet the prison representative. We stopped, but didn't see anyone around. While I studied the map and tried to decide what to do, the predawn light revealed that we were on the outskirts of Nuremberg. I had missed the intersection, and we had driven too far. Now, I had two choices: back track to the intersection and hope our escort was still there or try to find the prison on our own. I decided on the latter for two reasons. We were hours late, and I doubted that the escort would still be waiting. Second, I knew that Nuremberg, like every German city, was patrolled by M.P.'s twenty-four hours a day. I was sure that once we were in the city, we would see a patrol who could give us directions to the Palace of Justice.

I knew that I was not following procedure when I led the convoy into the city. No one was on the streets, however, I drove to what I thought was the center of the city and stopped. After about ten minutes I spotted two M.P.'s in a jeep driving on a cross street. I blew my horn and waved; they drove up to my jeep. One of the men glanced at the loads on the semis and at the code Numbers on the bumpers; the other asked if we were having trouble.

"Well, we're lost," I said. "We need to get to the Palace of Justice."

"What are you carrying?" the other MP asked.

"Lumber," I said. "Could you escort us in?" I hoped that they wouldn't ask why a convoy from the Nuremberg depot was lost in Nuremberg.

"The Palace is out of our sector, and we're going off duty. Soon as we get back to our headquarters we'll send someone who can take you in."

I was about to protest. but decided it would only raise their suspicions. Besides, the M.P.'s were wet from the rain and had to be cold and tired. I agreed and thanked them for their trouble.

We all climbed out to stretch and have a cigarette. The drivers checked their air hoses and ropes. I talked to Woods for a minute and told him why I had decided not to return to the intersection. He said that he was for anything that would get us to the Palace.

Before I finished my second cigarette a jeep with two M.P.'s appeared. They explained that they were dispatched to escort us to the Palace and would do so as soon as we were ready. I relaxed; we had made it, and I was certain that nothing else could go wrong.

CHAPTER ELEVEN

The Prison

In about twenty minutes we arrived at the Palace which was an impressive building that had six wings in a pattern that resembled a double "H." Each wing had five stories and a steep garroted roof. The prison was in a walled area behind the Palace and was not visible from the street.

I had been instructed by Colonel Clayton to enter a specific gate in the prison wall. The M.P. at the gate had apparently been alerted to our arrival. When I told him that I was Lieutenant Tilles from Landsberg, he immediately opened the gate.

When I saw the opening, I knew that I had relaxed too soon. It was narrow, and I didn't think the semis would fit. I spoke to the lead driver; he looked at the gate and walked to the rear of his truck to examine his load. Finally, he took a length of rope and measured both the gate and the load.

"Probably have an inch or two clearance. Not much," he reported to me.

"You think you can make it?" I asked.

"Is there an alternative?"

"Carry everything in on our backs," I said.

"In that case we'll make it."

It took some time, nearly forty minutes and much backing and jockeying, but all three trucks cleared the gate. The edge of one platform scraped the side of the gate for several feet, but no damage was done. Directly inside the gate was a courtyard and the gymnasium where the executions would be held. Both the courtyard and the gym were regular exercise areas for the soldiers stationed at the prison, but now the area was restricted and all the exercise equipment had been removed.

We unloaded the trucks and reported to our respective areas. The drivers moved the trucks to the transit barracks where the drivers would be billeted until their services were needed to remove the gallows. Woods and the men reported to the commander of the security detachment of the prison and were assigned quarters at the security barracks. They were issued two passes; one for admission to the Palace of Justice itself, and the other, and by far the more exclusive, for admission to the gymnasium. I reported to Major Teich, the liaison officer for Colonel Andrus. I expected to be chewed out; I had violated several of my orders. I had missed the intersection; entered Nuremberg unescorted; entered in daylight hours, and had asked for directions. To my surprise Major Teich warmly welcomed me into his office and made no mention of my indiscretions beyond the fact that his man at the intersection had become worried about us. Teich was pleased that we had made it safely and with enough time to prepare the gallows. He told me to get my room at the Grand Hotel and to report back to him at 0800 hours the next morning, October 15th. I told him that my men would begin assembling the gallows that afternoon and I wanted to be present. Teich agreed, issued me my passes, and ordered a jeep and driver to take me to the Grand.

The Grand Hotel was a few blocks from the Palace and in pre-war Germany it had lived up to its name and had hosted

123

dignitaries for all of Europe. Hitler had his own suite there and many meetings involving top level Nazis were conducted at the Grand. The lobby, with its sweeping stair case, columns, mezzanine balconies, and marble appointments still maintained its stature despite the drop clothes and tarps that covered areas that were under repair. The dining room, where I ate an early lunch, had lost most of its elegance. The glittering table settings and flatware that had held the gourmet dishes to satisfy the tastes of aristocrats had been replaced with more utilitarian ware designed to serve the principals of the trial. I remember that food tasted exceptionally good, but I had been up all night and was famished.

After lunch, I went to my room, which was rather plain, but it had a private bath and plenty of hot water. I arranged for a driver to take me back to the Palace at 1600 hours, luxuriated in a hot shower, fell on the bed, and immediately went to sleep.

When I rejoined the men in the gymnasium later that afternoon, they had already begun the assembly of the gallows. Under Woods' direction all the windows were blacked out. This was done so that our work could be completed in privacy, but it also established the somber setting of the execution chamber. A long, black curtain had been hung in front of the basketball goal on the right side of the gym. The curtain hid the eleven wooden coffins that sat behind it. After a dinner break the men resumed the assembly and completed all three gallows in the early morning hours of October 15th. As Woods had predicted, the task took about eleven hours.

At 0800 hours on October 15th, Woods and I sat in Major Teich's office. The major was visibly upset, and our report that the gallows were ready did little to calm him. The Soviets, he explained, had made a last minute request to inspect the gallows and wanted to witness a mock hanging, which Teich assumed meant a sand filled duffel bag dropping through the trap door. Teich said that the Soviets had been a source of problems since the formation of the Tribunal. They made difficult demands, cared little about the constraints of logistics, and were hopelessly stubborn. He warned that the slightest error or misunderstanding during our demonstration could result in the Soviets declaring the gallows unsuitable which would delay the executions indefinitely. No one, Teich emphasized, would be happy with such a delay. He told me to return to his office at 1300 hours and Woods to be ready in the gymnasium for a demonstration.

I understood Teich's meaning and knew that our demonstration had to be perfect. Outside the office I asked Woods if everything was ready and if the men need some practice run throughs.

Woods seemed unconcerned. "We are ready, Lieutenant. The men have been up for two nights. I'm letting them rest. We'll do just fine.

I wasn't as confident as Woods, but there wasn't much I could do except worry. I went back to the Grand, had lunch, and lounged in the lobby. At 1300 hours I presented myself to Major Teich, and we waited for the Soviets.

A half hour later the Soviets arrived. I recognized the one who was obviously in charge as General Niktchenko. He was the Soviet representative on the Tribunal; two weeks before he had participated in the sentencing of the war criminals. We were going to be inspected by the top man. Niktchenko was tall, stern, and dressed in a tailored uniform bedecked with ribbons and medals. I saluted him and felt the sweat that had formed on my brow. The General offered his hand to both Teich and myself and introduced his companions who consisted of his aide, a medical doctor, and an interpreter. The interpreter, however, was mostly silent. Niktchenko spoke English, and although it was broken and accented, he was proud of his ability to converse in it. He relied on the interpreter only when he had forgotten a word.

Niktchenko and Teich exchanged pleasantries for a few minutes, each trying to avoid offending the other. Teich announced that the gallows were ready for inspection in the gymnasium, but due to a pressing appointment he couldn't attend. Lieutenant Tilles, he said, would accompany the general.

This was news to me. Teich and I had spent a half hour together waiting for the Soviets, and he had never mentioned an appointment. He may have had one, or he simply may have wished to distance himself from the inspection and demonstration in case something went wrong.

I managed to find my voice and invited the general and his companions to follow me to the gymnasium. We stepped into the courtyard, and the autumn air cooled the sweat that every pore of my body released. I hoped that I wouldn't say or do anything that would result in an international incident or make me look ridiculous.

Woods and Malta were waiting inside the gym, and they came to attention when we entered. I provided introductions, pronouncing the Russian names as well as I could, and Woods took charge. He directed the Soviets to the gallows he had rigged with a sand bag and began explaining its operation. I saw Niktchenko nodding, and I relaxed. Woods knew his craft and enjoyed showing off his handiwork. The Soviets spent over thirty minutes examining the gallows and directing each other's attention to various items. Woods was asked many questions, but he never faltered, and the Soviets nodded in agreement with all of his answers. Finally, Woods signaled Malta to mount the steps and pull the hangman's handle. The sand bag dropped with a thud, and the Soviets reflexively stepped back. Woods pointed out his device to latch the trap door open. The Soviets were impressed with this, and all four crowded under the platform to examine it. Woods happily showed how it worked. The Soviets smiled, nodded vigorously, and all four shook hands with Woods. Niktchenko led his companions to the exit, but he stopped to shake my hand and thank me. I asked the general if he wanted me to accompany him. He shook his head and wished us all well.

Woods strolled over to me, obviously pleased with himself. "Told you it would be fine, Lieutenant."

He was right; the Soviet inspection was the last hurdle. We were ready to hang the Nuremberg war criminals.

CHAPTER TWELVE

The Executions

I reported the results of the inspection to Major Teich later that afternoon. He was pleased, thanked me, and told me that we would receive our final instructions in a meeting scheduled for 2300 that night. Everyone involved with the hangings was ordered to be there. In the meantime, Teich requested that we stay within the confines of the Palace of Justice. I relayed that information to Woods and the men, we ate dinner together at the mess hall, and we waited.

While we waited the prisoners experienced a routine evening. A typical meal of sausage, black bread, and potato salad was served to each man in his cell at the regular time. The prisoners wrote letters and read until the lights were dimmed at 2100 hours as usual. von Ribbentrop expressed his normal complaints about noise and insomnia, and Rosenberg complained about his cold hands. Although the prisoners suspected that their executions were imminent, no one knew that October 15th was their last night on earth. Andrus purposefully withheld that information and maintained the prison routine until the last possible moment to avoid any protests, suicide attempts, or bids for final glory.

At 2200 hours Andrus went to each prisoner's cell and read his death order. He informed each man that his death would be in a matter of hours. The provision of the Geneva Convention that required that the condemned hear his death order twenty-four hours prior to his execution had been waved to maintain security and secrecy. According the Andrus' report each prisoner accepted his fate without emotion. Streicher inquired about the well being of the other prisoners; Keitel wished to be given time to set his cell in order; Seyss-Inquart said that he had been expecting it; Frick hoped that he wouldn't have long to wait; Sauckel still maintained that his conviction was an error, but accepted his fate. Confession and communion were arranged for the Catholics, Seyss-Inquart, Frank, and Kaltenbrunner. As Andrus made his way from cell to cell, Goering slipped a cyanide capsule into his mouth.

At 2300 hours Woods, the men, and I assembled in a wood paneled room. We sat on wooden folding chairs, sipped coffee, and waited for Major Teich to give us instructions. The door was guarded, and once we entered we were not allow to leave. There were about thirty of us in the room; most were soldiers. The others included eight members of the press, two from each country that comprised the Tribunal. Arthur Goeth and Kingsbury Smith represented the United States; Selkirk Parton and Basil Gingell were from Great Britain; France was represented by Louis DeRoche and Sacha Simon, and Major Antonvic and Captain Boris Vladimirovic represented the Soviet Union. Doctor Wilhelm Hoagner and Doctor Fredrich Leisner were the official German witnesses.

At 2330 hours Colonel Andrus opened the door and strode to the front of the room. Everyone stopped talking; Andrus had not been scheduled to conduct this meeting and his presence signaled something important. Andrus was an imposing figure. He was tall and crowned with a shellacked helmet that reflected the overhead lights. A silver eagle, the prison insignia, was emblazoned on the helmet's front; a riding crop was tucked under his left arm. Andrus was pale and his jaw muscles worked furiously. When he reached the front of the room, he turned and announced in a clear, but high pitched voice, "Gentlemen, Hermann Goering has committed suicide."

There was a stunned silence for several moments. Andrus stated that Goering's death had occurred at 2245 hours and was accomplished by ingesting poison. The executions, he added would continue on schedule.

The correspondents found their voices and peppered Andrus with questions about the specifics of the suicide. Andrus responded by stating the an investigation was being conducted and an official statement would be issued. One reporter asked for permission to leave and notify his paper. Andrus denied his request and stated that the information would not be made public until after the executions. That was his final point, and Andrus turned and left the room.

Andrus' demeanor, which was calm and professional, belied his inner turmoil. He and Goering had been adversaries since Goering had arrived at Bad Mondorf, and Goering had beaten him. Andrus had been unable to locate Goering's cyanide capsules, and he had been unable to deliver Goering to his execution. After Ley's suicide, Andrus had declared his prison to be "suicide proof." With just minutes remaining before the executions, which marked the end of Andrus' responsibility for the prisoners, Goering's suicide mocked him. In case Andrus missed the point, Goering left a note directed to Andrus declaring that he was more clever than his keeper. Goering's suicide weighed heavily enough on Andrus' mind that on his death bed nearly twenty years later among the last words he spoke were, "Goering has committed suicide. I must inform the council.

Major Teich took charge of the meeting and spent about twenty minutes outlining our procedure. A lieutenant colonel from the prison staff would escort each prisoner from his cell and through the corridor to the gymnasium door. He would knock on the door to indicate that he was ready. One of my M.P.'s would open the door, and the prisoner and the colonel would take three steps inside. The colonel would remove the prisoner's shackles and leave the chamber. At this point the prison staff relinquished responsibility for the prisoner to myself and the M.P.'s. Two of the M.P.'s would hold the prisoner by his arms; the two others would follow immediately behind. Two lieutenant colonels from the Provost Marshal Section Third Army would lead the prisoner to the gallows; a chaplain, either Protestant or Catholic depending on the prisoner's religion, and an interpreter would follow behind the M.P.'s. I would bring up the rear and complete the formation. The prisoner would be led to face the members of the Tribunal, and he would be asked to state his name. He would then be led to the thirteen steps to the gallows' platform. The two M.P.'s would take the prisoner up the stairs, still holding onto his arms. The other two M.P.'s would pass behind the gallows to retrieve a canvas stretcher that was behind the long, black curtain that separated the execution chamber from the coffins. When the prisoner was declared dead, the MP's would load his body onto the stretcher and place him on top of a pine coffin behind the curtain. When all the prisoners had been executed the official army photographers would take two pictures of each body resting on top of his coffin. These would be the only photographs of the executions that were permitted.

At 0025 hours on the morning of October 16th, Major Teich closed the meeting and admonished us not to leave our positions until all the executions were completed. He led us from the room and across the courtyard to the gymnasium. The night was cold, and the wind pierced our clothing and whipped the clouds into an angry sky that blotted the moon and stars. The M.P. at the door checked all of our passes as a prescribed formality. We entered the execution chamber, Major Teich switched on the overhead lights, and we blinked against their brightness. It was impossible not to see the gallows; they were huge, foreboding, and hopelessly out of place next to the basketball hoop at the end of the chamber. The two main gallows, the ones to be used, stood together and opposite and slightly to the left of the door through which the prisoners would enter. They would be the first things the prisoners saw when they entered the chamber. The third gallows, the one held in reserve, was also opposite the door but in the right corner of the chamber. Next to the reserve gallows the black curtain hid the coffins. To the left of the main gallows four folding tables and chairs for each member of the Tribunal were placed in a diagonal line. Four other folding tables, two on each side of the door accommodated the eight members of the press. Besides escorting the prisoners, I was to record the time that each prisoner dropped through the trap door and the time that he was declared dead. After we escorted the condemned man to the steps, I would stand to the left of the gallows and would wait for the prisoner to drop. I would note the time on yellow lined paper and then rejoin the formation. When the doctors, one American and one Russian, declared the man dead, I would note the time again.

After the doctors made their announcement, Malta would cut the man down, and the two M.P.'s would place him on the stretcher and carry him from the chamber. No rope would be used twice, and between the hangings Woods would secure a fresh rope to the steel eye bolt on the gallows cross bar.

After we entered the chamber everyone quietly moved to their proper positions and waited. At 0110 hours a loud knock on the door gave us a start. An M.P. opened the door and Joachim von Ribbentrop entered the chamber. He closed his eyes to the bright lights as his shackles were removed. He opened them and blinked and glanced around the room; his thin lips were set in a straight line. He walked without hesitation across the chamber with the M.P.'s holding his arms. When the Tribunal asked for his name, he shouted "Joachim von Ribbentrop," which was the only indication of his nervousness. He mounted the steps between the two M.P.'s and once on the platform, Woods turned him around to face us. He was asked if he had any last words, and he said, "God protect Germany." He asked if he could say something else. Permission was given, and he said, "My greatest wish is that Germany realizes its unity and that understanding be reached between the East and the West. I wish peace to the world."

After these words were translated into English, the interpreter, chaplain, and the M.P.'s descended the stairs. Woods placed the hood over von Ribbentrop's head and adjusted the noose around his neck. Malta tied his feet with an army web belt and his hands with a boot lace. Woods stepped back to the hangman's handle and waited for the signal from the Provost Marshal officer. It came quickly; von Ribbentrop dropped at 0116 hours.

While von Ribbentrop dangled, Field Marshall Wilhelm Keitel entered the chamber. He was, however, unable to see von Ribbentrop who was concealed behind a black curtain that covered the front and sides of the gallows. The gently swaying rope was the only evidence that a hanging was in progress.

Keitel walked the last few steps of his life as he had lived his entire adulthood, with military bearing and erectness. He crisply responded, "Wilhelm Keitel," when asked his name, and on the gallows he looked directly at the Tribunal and spoke his last words, "God Almighty have mercy on the German people. Two million German soldiers went to their deaths for the Fatherland. I will follow my sons." He shouted, "All for Germany." The M.P.'s, interpreter, and chaplain left the platform; Woods applied the hood and noose. At 0120 hours Keitel dropped through the trap door.

Both von Ribbentrop and Keitel were dangling, and the proceeding came to a halt until one was declared dead. We stood in awkward silence for several moments. One of the colonels from the Provost Marshall section asked the Tribunal if smoking could be permitted. The four members conferred briefly and granted permission; cigarettes appeared between almost every pair of lips. The chamber, although becoming smoke filled, was silent, eerily silent. I could hear the scratching of the reporters' fountain pens, the occasional scuff of a boot sole on the gym floor, the buzz from the overhead lights, and the groaning of the ropes. All seemed deafening.

At 0130 hours the doctors emerged from behind the curtain that concealed von Ribbentrop, and the American doctor said, "This man is dead." That announcement moved us to action. The two M.P.'s appeared with the stretcher, and Malta stepped behind the curtain to cut the body down. With the noose still around his neck and the hood still covering his face, von Ribbentrop was removed from the chamber. Woods secured a new rope, and the Provost Marshal officer signaled the prison officer to admit the next prisoner.

Ernst Kaltenbrunner entered the chamber at 0136 hours. He seemed a giant, but a haggard giant. His face was thin and the scars from his drunken accident were apparent. He was dressed in a blue suit over a knit sweater, possibly to warm him in the chilly weather. He seemed nervous and wet his lips several times, but walked steadily. He spoke his last words calmly and quietly, "I would like to say a word. I have loved my German people and my fatherland with a warm heart. I have done my duty by the laws of my people, and I was sorry my people were led this time by men who were not soldiers and that crimes were committed of which I had no knowledge." After Woods placed the hood over his head, Kaltenbrunner added, "Germany, good luck." At 0139 hours the only Nuremberg war criminal that actually took part in the killing of the Jews dropped to his death.

The doctor pronounced Keitel dead at 0133 hours; he was cut down, and the gallows were prepared for Alfred Rosenberg. Rosenberg did not look well when he entered the chamber. His cheeks were sunken and his complexion was pasty.

He walked slowly, deliberately placing one foot in front of the other as if walking were a new activity. He supplied his name, but had no last words. He was the only prisoners to die without speaking. Although Rosenberg was an atheist, the chaplain stood on the platform with him and prayed. Rosenberg stared straight ahead, ignoring the chaplain and everyone else. He dropped at 0149 hours.

With Kaltenbrunner and Rosenberg dangling the proceeding paused again. We were permitted to smoke, and we did so in silence. Kaltenbrunner was declared dead at 0152 hours, and four minutes later Hans Frank entered the chamber.

Frank was the only one of the condemned to enter with a smile on his face. He was nervous and his adam's apple bobbed as he swallowed constantly. He stated his name quietly and almost whispered his last statement, "I am thankful for the kind treatment during my captivity, and I ask God to accept me with mercy. He closed his eyes and waited for Woods to apply the hood and noose. He dropped at 0158:30 hours.

Seconds later at 0159 hours Rosenberg was declared dead and a new rope was affixed for Wilhelm Frick. Frick's face glistened with sweat as he crossed the chamber. He was one of the older prisoners and his walk was a halting shuffle. He stumbled on the thirteenth step of the gallows and would have fallen if the M.P.'s had not been holding his arms. His last words were, "Long live eternal Germany." He dropped at 0208 hours.

Hans Frank was pronounced dead at 0209 hours, and the gallows were prepared for Julius Streicher. Streicher was easily the most obnoxious prisoner, and he maintained that characteristic to the final moments of his life. He eyes shone as he fixed an angry, unrepentant glare on the Tribunal. His mouth twitched into a sneer as he approached their tables. Suddenly, Streicher jerked his right arm free from the M.P.'s grasp, raised it in the Nazi salute and screamed "Heil, Hitler" at the Tribunal. The MP immediately secured Streicher's arm, and he was asked his name. Streicher refused to reply and stated, "You know my name well." After several requests he finally shouted "Julius Streicher, and was led up the steps.

Everyone in the chamber had watched Streicher's performance and none of it was lost on Woods. I knew that Woods hated Germans and still nursed a sore spot for his friends killed at the Malmedy Massacre, and I watched his face become florid and his jaws clench. Streicher's last words did not improve Woods' disposition. As soon as he reached the platform Streicher screamed, "Now it goes to God." While his hands and feet were being tied he stared at the Tribunal and shouted "Purim Fest, 1946." (Purim is a Jewish holiday commemorating the hanging of Haman, the biblical oppressor of the Jews.) He followed this with, "The Bolsheviks will hang you one day." Woods applied the hood and Streicher, knowing he would live only moments more softly said, "Adele, my dear wife." Woods adjusted the noose, but placed its coils off center. would not snap Streicher's neck, and he'd strangle. I realized instantly that this was Woods' intent, and I saw a small smile cross his lips as he pulled the hangman's handle. Streicher dropped at 0214 hours, and unlike the other men who died soundlessly, Streicher's gasps and gurgles filled the chamber. Everyone heard his gasps, and everyone denied hearing them. No one moved to Streicher's aid, no one objected, no one uttered any type of comment. Streicher had so angered the Tribunal, the prison staff, and finally his executioner that he was denied a painless death. His gasps ceased, and he was declared dead at 0223 hours.

Minutes before Streicher was pronounced dead, Frick's body had been cut down and removed. Fritz Sauckel entered the chamber at 0224 hours. He had been described as confused during the trial, and he was still confused. He had to be forced to dress for his final walk, and he seemed disoriented in the chamber. He looked wildly around the room and finally fixed his gaze on the Tribunal, men that he probably recognized from the trial. He wailed, "I am dying an innocent man. The sentence is wrong." On the platform he said, "I pay my respects to U. S. soldiers and officers, but not to U.S. justice." Some people believed he said "U.S. Jews" rather than U.S. justice, but I believe that he said

justice. His last words were, "God protect Germany and make Germany great again. Long live Germany. God protect my family." Sauckel dropped at 0226 hours and probably never understood why he needed to die.

Streicher was cut down and removed, and General Alfred Jodl entered at 0230 hours. He was in uniform, but the collar of his coat was askew, as if he had hurriedly put it on. Jodl's normally pinched face looked drawn, and he wet his thin lips continually. His plodded across the chamber, and the M.P.'s supported him. His final words, "My greetings to you, my Germany," were said clearly and loudly. He dropped at 0234 hours. Jodl dangled the longest of the men: a full sixteen minutes passed before the doctors declared him dead.

Sauckel was cut down, and the last prisoner, Arthur Seyss-Inquart entered at 0238:30 hours. He wore his thick glasses and limped on his damaged foot. He lurched and lost his balance when he stated his name, and he was held erect by the M.P.'s. He mounted the steps slowly and relied on the support of the M.P.'s. He said his last words in a low voice, "I hope that this execution is the last act of tragedy of the Second World War and that the lesson taken from this world war be that peace and understanding should exist between people. I believe in Germany." Woods applied the hood, adjusted the noose, and the last condemned Nuremberg war criminal dropped to his death at 0245 hours.

While Jodl and Seyss-Inquart were still dangling two

prison guards carried the body of Hermann Goering into the chamber on a stretcher and placed it between the gallows. He was covered with an army blanket, but his bare feet with tightly curled toes protruded. A Provost Marshall officer ordered the blanket removed so that the Tribunal, the witnesses, and correspondents could see that Goering was indeed dead. The army wanted to thwart any type of rumor that Goering had escaped.

Goering was clad in black silk pajamas, the tops of which were still wet from attempts to revive him. His face was contorted into the visage of a gargoyle and his skin had a greenish tint. Goering had wanted to cheat the hangman and defy his judges, and he did. He believed that a hanging death was an insult; suicide was more honorable. His twisted features revealed that in order to have his honorable death, Goering had spent his last moments of life in agony.

Goering's body was removed to his coffin behind the black curtain and the Tribunal announced. "These proceedings are closed," and the men exited the chamber along with the correspondents, interpreters, doctors, and chaplains. The executions ended at 0257 hours and had lasted for one hour and forty one minutes.

The only personnel in the chamber were Woods, myself, our MP's, and a detail of a half dozen prison guards. The prison guards removed the black curtain and accompanied the army photographers as they took two pictures of each of the condemned. The condemned still rested on top of their coffins: their hoods had been removed, but each still had his noose fixed around his neck. One picture was taken of the men in their clothing; one was taken of them naked. These pictures were sent to the Allied Control Council in Berlin. No pictures of the chamber or the personnel were allowed.

138

When the photographers had finished they were escorted from the chamber, and the prison guards placed the bodies into the coffins and nailed the lids shut. They loaded the coffins into two covered trucks that were waiting in the courtyard. The trucks were escorted from the prison by two jeeps, each of which was equipped with a mounted machine gun that was manned by an M.P. They left Nuremberg via a planned route of streets that were blocked off by military police. Outside Nuremberg they took a circuitous route to Munich. Although the trucks left the Palace of Justice at about 0400 hours, no announcement of their departure or of the completion of the executions were made until three hours later. The army wanted to prevent any chance that fanatical Nazis might try to commandeer the bodies. In Munich the crematorium facilities of a private mortuary were pressed into service and all eleven war criminals were cremated. I thought that it would have been more fitting to cremate them in the ovens at Treblinka or Auschwitz, but that would not have been practical.

While the prison detail removed the bodies, Woods and our men disassembled the gallows and loaded them onto the semis that had brought them. This took about four hours; when we finished I personally thanked all the men and complimented them on their professionalism in a difficult assignment. The men accompanied the gallows to Landsberg prison. They were burned the next day to prevent anyone from collecting souvenirs. Woods and I shook hands and were both saddened by the fact that we would probably not see each other again. Woods joined the press contingent at the prison and was interviewed by correspondents from across the globe; he maintained his pride in his craft throughout the interview.

I was the last man to leave the execution chamber. It had reverted to a gymnasium again. A few scuff marks on the floor were the only indication that men had paid with their lives for their participation in the most heinous regime in modern times. I pulled the door closed and blinked against the morning sun.

CHAPTER THIRTEEN

After the Executions

I returned to the Grand Hotel, packed my gear, and drove to Heidelberg, the post to which I was regularly assigned, and prepared to leave Germany. Part of those preparations included selling my jeep which I hated to do, but I wanted a decent American car when I returned to the states. A week later I boarded a ship at Bremerhaven, Germany for the trip home. I don't know if it was the anticipation of joining my family, a release of tension after the executions or simple seasickness, but I threw up during the entire trip.

After I was processed at Fort Dix I was reunited with my family, and I experienced the bliss enjoyed by thousands of G.I.'s who once again saw their loved ones. For several hours the world was shut out and there was only my wife, my son, and myself. My wife and I learned why we had fallen in love and fell in love again. My son had grown and was no longer a toddler and was shy around me at first. After a couple of days he was used to me again; we played catch, and I watched him ride his bicycle. My wife and I spent hours touching, holding each other. Those first days after my return home were the most intensely happy and pleasure filled days of my life.

I wanted no more part of the army; I was tired of uniforms and orders, and I never wanted to be away from my family again. However, I was convinced, along with most other Americans, that a war with the Soviet Union was inevitable. If I left the army, I would lose my commission, and if war started, I would be inducted as an enlisted man. If I joined the army reserves, I could keep my commission. After several discussions with my wife, I decided to join the reserves. The conflict with the Soviets never escalated past the cold war stage, which made my decision moot. I stayed in the reserves until 1978 when I retired with the rank of Lieutenant Colonel. The reserves didn't save me from combat, but they helped me retire comfortably.

I never spoke much about the executions; only my family and a few close friends knew of my involvement. I suppose that I felt like most other people; the war was over, and we wanted everything to be normal again. I'm sure that the executions changed my life in some way, but only in the way that any event changes a person's life. I went back to my job at the A. S. Browne Company and tried to provide a good life for my family. I didn't dream of falling bodies, and I wasn't racked with guilt. The army had given me a job, and I had done it. I took Wood's advice--I didn't worry about the men that I helped hang. Their fates were determined by their lives and their judges.

After his interview Woods returned to Third Army Headquarters. He applied for retirement, and some months later he became a civilian employee of the army. We lost touch, but in the early 1950's I read in the paper that he had been killed in the Marianna Islands. A high voltage wire had fallen and electrocuted him. I always thought it ironic that Woods, who took great pride in his skills as a hangman, and who, by his estimation, held the record for hanging the most men, a total of 347, had met his end through electrocution.

For some reason, perhaps because of his forthright answers during his interview or because he was an easy scapegoat for what some felt were unjust sentences by the Tribunal, the press was not kind to Woods. Cecil Catling of the London Star was especially scathing in his report. For some reason he believed that the men took too long to die; he stated that Keitel took twenty-eight minutes to die. He reported that the men's faces had been smashed and that all the men emitted horrible noises after they dropped. He stated that the men had not been properly tied and had not fallen from a sufficient height. All had died from strangulation, not from having their necks snapped. Later accounts of the executions used Catling's opinions and the fact that the army did not use Woods as a hangman after Nuremberg as evidence that Woods bungled the executions. One account of the executions maintained that Woods left the platform and went behind the curtain with a small club in his hand implying that he beat the men to death. Another account omitted Woods' involvement completely.

None of Woods' detractors were in the execution chamber; none witnessed the hangings, or saw the gallows. I am one of the last men alive who was actually in the execution chamber, and I can defend Woods' performance. No man hung for twenty-eight minutes as Catling said. I kept the times of death for each of the men, and I still have the original paper on which I recorded the times. Jodl dangled the longest, sixteen minutes, a time that is not extraordinary. Most of the men expired in ten to twelve minutes, which is the usual amount of time. Woods never left the platform of the gallows; he never had a club, and he never stepped behind the gallows curtain. Such things would never have been permitted by the Tribunal. The only persons who went behind the curtain were the doctors who pronounced the men dead and Malta who cut them down. Any blood or discoloration on the men's face in the army photographs, some of which were reproduced in newspapers and magazines several weeks after the executions, were the natural results of hanging. The condemned frequently bite through their lips and tongues and the pressure from the rope can cause hemorrhages. Woods stumbled on a question about this during his interview which led to more conjecture that he botched the job. Woods probably stumbled over the question because he never saw the men after they dropped. He had no interest in viewing their corpses as they were photographed, and he kept his attention on directing the men as they disassembled the gallows. His only interest in the condemned was that they dropped properly, and they did. The army did not use Woods again because he retired, not because his competence was questioned.

The only exception to what I have stated would be the hanging of Julius Streicher. That was the only time that I saw Woods exhibit any emotion during a hanging. Streicher's outburst angered Woods, and Woods punished him for it. Everyone in the chamber knew exactly what Woods had done, and no one objected.

To my knowledge Woods never bothered to defend himself against the allocations that he performed poorly. He may have not known how, but, knowing Woods, he simply didn't care. He knew that his hangings were proper and that was all that matter to him. He never attempted to glorify his participation or reap rewards from his role in the executions. He had done his job and had done it well.

A few days after the bodies of the war criminals were cremated at Munich I understand that their ashes were scattered from a plane over Berlin. The last architects of the Thousand Year Reich, The Perfect Society, The Master Race, became dust in the wind.

References

"The Dawn without Tears," Time, October 28, 1946.

deZayas, Alfred. The Wehrmacht War Crimes Bureau, 1939-1945. Lincoln: University of Nebraska Press, 1989.

Gutman, Israel, ed. Encyclopedia of the Holocaust. New York: McMillan Publishing, 1990.

"A German war Criminal Pays the Penalty for his Acts," New York Times, May 30, 1946.

Harris, Whitney. Tyranny on Trial. Dallas: Southern Methodist University Press. 1954

"Last of the Dachau Condemned to Die," Los Angeles Times, May 30, 1946

"Little Caesar," Time, December 31, 1945.

"Nazi Crimes from A to Z," Newsweek, December 24, 1945.

"Night without Dawn," Time, October 28, 1946.

Persico, Joseph E. Nuremberg, Infamy on Trial. New York: Penguin Books, 1994.

Smith, Marcus. Dachau: The Harrowing Hell. Albany: State University of New York Press, 1995.

"Trial of the Small Fry," Newsweek, June 11, 1945.

United Nations War Crimes Commission. Law Reports of Trials of War Criminals, Vol. XI. London: His Majesty's Stationer Office, 1948

Other Titles from JoNa Books

ISBN 0-9657929-0-0. Jim Peters: Texas Ranger by Lee Paul. Follow this living legend on some of the most famous criminal cases in Texas history. 216 pages. $12.95.

ISBN 0-9657929-1-9. Pacific Empire by G. Miki Hayden. Nine interconnecting stories of Japanese victory in World War II. An alternate history. 1998 New York Times recommended summer reading. 200 pages. $12.95

ISBN 0-9657929-3-5. Gesundheit, Dummy! The Best of Baloo by Rex May. One of America's leading cartoonists brings his first collected works to book form. 88 pages. $7.95.

Books can be ordered from your local bookstore, or by adding $2.00 for postage and handling per book to:

JoNa Books
P. O. Box 336
Bedford, IN 47421

Check our web site for upcoming releases and news from JoNa Books. http://www.kiva.net/~jonabook.